Contents

Acknowledgements

This book is the outcome of several years' committed work from a number of people. We should like to thank in particular the heads and teachers involved in the study, and their LEA minders, for being so generous with their time and ideas. The research project could not have run without the support and organisation skills of Susan Stocker who was also responsible for transcribing all the tapes and for the initial preparation of the manuscript. The final manuscript was produced with skill and patience by Ann Popham and Jason McKenzie, to whom the first author owes particular thanks. We must also acknowledge our debt to Anna Clarkson who had the temerity to suggest that we try and turn a research report into a good read; we hope that we have achieved just that. Finally, we thank the Economic and Social Research Council for funding, over a total of eight years, and for a regime which allows longer term creative research to flourish.

What Makes a Good Primary School Teacher?

We know that successful teachers need to use a range of teaching strategies, but what are they? *What Makes a Good Primary School Teacher?* provides a fascinating account of the range of teaching, assessment and feedback strategies used by individual 'expert' teachers.

The book describes:

- the most common lesson patterns, why and when they are used;

- how teaching strategies are varied according to subjects;

- how assessment and feedback information can encourage pupils to learn;

- the differences in teaching seven-year-olds and eleven-year-olds.

This accessible and concise book illustrates good teaching practice. Based on extensive fieldwork by respected researchers and authors, *What Makes a Good Primary School Teacher?* contains case study excerpts and quotes from teachers. It will be an essential read for all students about to embark on primary teacher training courses, and of great interest to experienced practitioners.

Caroline Gipps is Deputy Vice-Chancellor at Kingston University. She has written *Beyond Testing – Towards a Theory of Educational Assessment* published by Falmer Press. **Bet McCallum** is an educational researcher at the Institute of Education, London. She has been involved in research with Caroline Gipps on the introduction of National Assessment, teachers' assessment practice and the assessment, teaching and feedback strategies of primary teachers.
Eleanore Hargreaves is a lecturer in evaluation and assessment and a research officer at the Institute of Education, London.

What Makes a Good Primary School Teacher?

Expert classroom strategies

Caroline Gipps, Bet McCallum and Eleanore Hargreaves

London and New York

First published 2000 by RoutledgeFalmer
11 New Fetter Lane, London EC4P 4EE

Simultaneously published in the USA and Canada
by RoutledgeFalmer
29 West 35th Street, New York, NY 10001

RoutledgeFalmer is an imprint of the Taylor & Francis Group

Typeset in 10/12pt Goudy by Graphicraft Limited, Hong Kong
Printed and bound in Great Britain by Clays Ltd, St Ives plc

British Library Cataloguing in Publication Data
A catalogue record for this book is available from the British Library

Library of Congress Cataloging in Publication Data
Gipps, C. V.
    What makes a good primary school teacher? : expert classroom strategies /
Caroline Gipps, Bet McCallum, and Eleanore Hargreaves.
        p.   cm.
    Includes bibliographical references index.
    1. Elementary school teaching—Great Britain—Case studies.   2. Effective
teaching—Great Britain—Case studies.   I. McCallum, Bet, 1943–   II. Hargreaves,
Eleanore, 1961–   III. Title.
LB1555.G56   2001
372.1102—dc21   00-034478

ISBN 0-415-23246-5 (hbk)
ISBN 0-415-23247-3 (pbk)

Chapter 1

Setting the scene

INTRODUCTION

Twenty-eight seven-year-olds were sitting at the feet of their teacher, looking up expectantly. She had a tray of objects on her lap and was picking them up one at a time and examining them carefully without a word – a Victorian doll, a Brownie camera, a green glass bottle stopper, a locket, a watch, a fossil.

She posed a question . . . *'What is history?'*. A voice from the floor suggested *'in the past'*. *'How long ago is in the past?'* asked the teacher. Answers ranged from *'The Romans'* to *'when my granny lived'* to *'a minute ago'*. All the contributions were accepted and the teacher used them to explain that people's memories can be used to find out about the past and objects can be carefully examined because they contain clues about the past. Picking up the Brownie, she pointed it at individuals, looking through the viewfinder and making them smile. She modelled how to examine an object, giving a running commentary on her conclusions about the characteristics of the Brownie, the materials it was made of, whether there was a date anywhere and how it was different from the class's new Olympus camera.

'The other day I was digging in my garden and I found something interesting . . .' reported the teacher. She paused just long enough to sustain attention . . . and then from her pocket produced a shard of patterned blue and white pottery.

'So I thought to myself – What had it come from? Who had it belonged to? I was very interested in this. So what did I do? I looked in a book and I found some examples with very similar designs. They were made by a man called Josiah Wedgewood . . .'

Before long the children set to work. In pairs they chose an object, described it in writing, drawing or diagram, looked for clues as to whether it was just *'old'* or *'very old'*, and guessed at its use. There were plenty of objects to go round and many of them were of great interest to the children – some of whom collected magnifiers from a resource cupboard to help them in their investigations.

During this part of the lesson, the teacher circulated, listening in to the conversation of pairs and joining in, often repeating some of her earlier questions – *'Well what is that made of do you think?'* – *'Who do you think may have owned it?'*

The teacher paced the lesson so that there was time at the end for the class to come together. She invited some children to make a presentation on their theories: everyone listened and commented, and the teacher gave praise to all concerned.

This is a real example of an experienced primary teacher giving a 'lesson'. In this, although it may not seem so to an outsider, she starts off with 'teaching', while during the middle of the lesson she is making assessments, giving feedback to individuals or groups. In the plenary at the end she is recapping, making connections, encouraging the children to explain and present, again making assessments and feeding back to the class as a whole.

Take another example.

At the other end of the school, 30 Y6 children came filing back into the classroom after break. They quickly settled into their groups of four. They were not arranged by ability but the teacher often moved particular children to work in certain groups – especially children who were good at explaining things to others. This did not happen today as it was to be a whole class lesson with everyone facing the board. Their science books were already stacked in the middle of the table and they quickly found their own and looked towards the teacher.

From the start the teacher explained that this would be a short, 30-minute lesson. She wanted to teach them something they would all need to know and use: that science often involves recording information on a chart and that she would show them one type of chart they could use over and over again.

The teacher instructed the children to look in their books and find reports they had done previously on 'properties of materials'; they were to refer to this as the lesson proceeded. The teacher invited contributions to help recap the work on materials – 'What kinds of things were we considering in that lesson?' – and the children explained that they had taken an object and had been considering how well the materials it was made of fitted its purpose. The teacher received all answers as valid and praised them. As part of the recap, the teacher sometimes used 'nonsense' scenarios to draw out children's understanding of appropriateness of materials – 'Why is a skipping rope not made of wood?'. Children were encouraged to theorise and talk freely and there was a lot of humour in the lesson.

Ten minutes into the lesson, the teacher repeated the purpose of the session: 'to draw up a clear chart in order to use it to make comparisons of different materials'.

The teacher demonstrated the idea of a chart or grid by drawing an empty grid on the board. She asked one individual to imagine a saucepan and asked what it might mostly be made of. Taking the child's answer ('metal') she invited contributions from the class – 'What can we say about metal?'. All answers were then accepted: 'hard'; 'inflammable'; 'opaque'. The teacher explained that not all the objects they had studied were hard, inflammable or opaque and to compare and contrast them they would need a format. She quizzed them for the opposites of 'hard'; 'inflammable'; 'opaque'. Hands shot up and children were keen to answer.

The teacher illustrated the idea of column heading by writing up as headings: 'hard', 'soft', 'inflammable', 'does not catch fire', 'opaque', 'transparent'. Down the side of the chart, she wrote the names of materials: 'metal', 'plastic', 'rubber', 'glass', and then asked the children whether each was 'hard' or 'soft', 'opaque' or 'transparent' and so on. She put ticks and crosses in the columns according to the answers to these questions.

The teacher tested out the children's understanding by asking about other objects in the room such as tables, pencils and books. Individuals made a few mistakes and the teacher's way of dealing with this was to tell them when they were wrong, ask them to think again or move on to ask another child.

Before ending the lesson, the teacher repeated that they should have a go at drawing up grids and use them regularly to display information they discovered.

Books were closed and it was time for music.

These two rather different examples offer us an insight into the range of activity that makes up good primary teaching practice. Teaching is a diverse, complex activity with no clear 'rules' except that the teacher should teach and the child should learn. So how do we make sense of such a diverse activity – how do we 'unpack' it? What advice do we give to new teachers to help them become good classroom teachers?

This book attempts to give good practical advice to teachers by unpacking and explaining some of the strategies used by experienced 'expert' teachers. In it we look at some of the key questions about primary school teaching. How do good teachers teach? What are the teaching strategies they use? How do they build assessment and feedback into the teaching/learning cycle? How does their teaching relate to how children learn? What are the differences between teaching seven-year-olds and teaching eleven-year-olds?

The book is based on research which we carried out with primary teachers in the late 1990s.[1] The 1990s saw a range of reports and advice to primary teachers about how to teach. The first of these, the 'Three Wise Men' Report on primary education urged teachers to operate in terms of a repertoire of approaches:

> These include: explaining, instructing, questioning, observing, assessing, diagnosing and providing feedback.
>
> (Alexander, Rose and Woodhead, 1992 p. 35)

The effective teacher has a range of

> organisational strategies and teaching techniques . . . [and] selects
> from this pedagogical repertoire according to the unique practical
> needs and circumstances of his or her professional situation rather
> than the dictates of educational fashion, ideology or habit.
>
> (Alexander, 1995 p. 2)

In 1997 the advice was to spend time on whole-class teaching (Reynolds, TES 26 June 1997) with the Chief Inspector proposing that whole-class teaching should be used for 50 per cent of teaching time, and more in mathematics. The statutory requirements for primary teacher training (Circular 4/98) states that trainees must demonstrate that they:

> ensure effective teaching of whole classes, and of groups and indi-
> viduals within the whole class setting, so that teaching objectives
> are met, and best use is made of available teaching time.

As we wrote this book, schools were introducing the literacy hour and the numeracy hour. These involve structured teaching of literacy and numeracy using various teaching strategies and prepared materials. So, primary teachers have received, through the 1990s, a considerable amount of exhortation and advice, but unfortunately, until recently not so much practical guidance.

We know from research that teachers tend to operate with a broad range of teaching approaches but we have little understanding of what range of strategies individual teachers use; how they know or decide which technique to bring into play and when; while assessment and feedback, which are key aspects of teaching, are rarely looked at as an integral part of the teaching process. It seemed to us that urging teachers to use a range of approaches with no guidance on what might be appropriate in different circumstances was not particularly helpful, so we developed a research project that would allow us to provide some of this advice, by studying the teaching, assessment and feedback practice of good primary teachers.

In this book we have tried to present what we found in a clear and meaningful way. We have grouped and categorised the various teaching, assessment and feedback strategies, given examples and used teachers' own words as far as possible. What we hope is that the examples and explanations in these pages will help student teachers and beginning teachers to develop their practice, and more experienced teachers to reflect on teaching and learning, and perhaps to try new approaches.

But first let us go back, to see what research *can* tell us about the key issues that we shall address in this book: teaching and learning, assessment and feedback. This will provide a frame for the picture we shall paint.

ASSESSMENT AND FEEDBACK

As the quote from the 'Three Wise Men' Report makes clear, assessing and providing feedback are key elements of teachers' practice. And yet, in many research studies, as in guidance to teachers, the three aspects (teaching, assessment and feedback) are kept separate. In our earlier research looking at the introduction of national assessment into primary schools (Gipps, Brown, McCallum and McAlister, 1995)[2] we became more and more convinced of the importance of teachers' informal assessment in the teaching process. What we mean by informal teacher assessment is when the teacher poses questions, observes children in activities, and evaluates pupils' work in a planned and systematic, or ad hoc, way. Repeating assessment of this sort, over a period of time, and in a range of contexts allows the teacher to build up a solid and broad-based understanding of what pupils have learned and can do. This sort of assessment is often called formative assessment. Formative assessment involves using assessment information to feed back into the teaching/learning process; some observers believe that assessment is only truly formative if it involves the pupil, although the more general understanding has been that the process mainly involves the teacher who uses the information to feed back into her planning. In teaching terms this means teachers using assessment information to feed back into the teaching process, and to determine for individuals or groups whether to explain the task again, to give further practise on it, or move onto the next stage.

But, in formative assessment teachers' judgements about children's learning and understanding can also be used to improve the learning process (rather than to provide grades or marks) by giving feedback to the learner directly; feedback about what is going well or done well, what is not right and how it can be improved. Without this sort of feedback the learner does not know what he or she needs to do to improve or get to the next stage. If teachers do not provide this sort of feedback then the learner is operating on a trial-and-error basis. As an Australian researcher Royce Sadler put it:

> Formative assessment is concerned with how judgements about
> the quality of student responses . . . can be used to shape and improve
> the student's competence by short-circuiting the randomness and
> inefficiency of trial-and-error learning.
>
> (Sadler, 1989 p. 120)

We found Sadler's work on formative assessment particularly valuable
as it helped us to locate informal assessment in the teaching/learning
cycle. Sadler's work on formative assessment stems from the 'common
but puzzling' observation that, even when teachers give learners valid
and reliable judgements or grades about their work, improvement does
not necessarily follow. But the point is that the learner needs more
than grades or marks to improve. In order for the learner to improve
she must have a notion of the performance, standard or goal the teacher
has in mind in order to be able to compare her actual performance
with the desired performance, and to engage in appropriate action to
'close the gap' between the two. Feedback from the teacher which
helps the learner needs to be of the kind and detail which tells the
student what to do to improve; the use of grades alone or 'good, 7/10'
marking cannot do this. Grades may in fact shift attention away from
learning and improvement, and be counter-productive for formative
purposes (Black and William, 1998).

In our earlier research on teacher feedback[3] we developed a classification, or typology, of teacher feedback in Year 1 and Year 2 classes
that was grounded in classroom practice (Tunstall and Gipps, 1996).
Briefly, apart from feedback used for socialisation purposes, feedback
from assessment can be classified as broadly evaluative, (aimed at main-
taining motivation and self-esteem) or descriptive (making specific
reference to achievement or competence in relation to the task at hand
or more general goals). This descriptive feedback often follows formative
assessment and offers pupils the information needed to 'close the gap'
between actual performance and desired performance. It is thus a crucial
element of any teaching repertoire.

TEACHING AND LEARNING

We also looked to see what research on learning theory could tell
us about teaching. We found that a significant shift has occurred
over the last 15 years in understanding how learning takes place. The

traditional view of learning is that learners 'absorb' new material in some way. This has supported a traditional view of teaching in which the teacher transmits information (as new material or facts) and the learner absorbs it. This approach is caricatured as a 'transmission' model with the learner as an empty vessel or blank slate ready to receive information, the speed with which they absorb it being determined by their intelligence. Here, learning is seen essentially as a passive process on the part of the learner. This is of course a caricature, as even the most traditional of teachers and the most passive of learners will engage in question and answer to clarify material when the learner clearly does not understand.

However, research in cognitive psychology has shown learning as a more active process. This work suggests that we see learning in terms of developing networks, with connections in many directions, not of an external map that is transposed directly into the student's head. This suggests that learning is a process of knowledge construction, an organic process of reorganising and restructuring as the student learns (Driver, Guesne and Tiberghien, 1985). If learning does occur, not by recording information, but by interpreting it, then teaching needs to be seen not as direct transfer of knowledge but as an intervention in an ongoing knowledge-construction process (Resnick, 1989). According to this *constructivist* learning theory, students learn by actively making sense of new knowledge, making meaning from it, and mapping it in to their existing knowledge maps or schema in their brains. The *social constructivist* approach recognises the importance of the social setting of learning (Driver, Asoko, Leach, Mortimer and Scott, 1994) and focuses on the individual acquiring knowledge within the social setting and culture of the classroom. Another theory of learning, the *sociocultural*, builds on Vygotsky's arguments about the importance of interaction with more knowledgeable others in learning, and the role of society in providing a framework for the child's learning; it therefore describes learning as essentially a social activity. As Bruner and Haste put it

> ... through ... social life, the child acquires a framework for interpreting experience and learns how to negotiate meaning in a manner congruent with the requirements of the culture. 'Making sense' is a social process; it is an activity that is always situated in a cultural and historical context.
>
> (Bruner and Haste, 1987 p. 1)

Furthermore, socioculturalists argue that meaning derived from inter-actions is not exclusive to the person learning: all participants can gain meaning and develop as a result of the learning interaction, in other words that teachers also learn while pupils are learning.

Given these different views, most constructivist and sociocultural theorists approach research on learning in different ways and disagree over whether learning, or coming to know, 'is located in the head or in the individual-in-social-action' (Cobb, 1994 p. 13). Vygotsky's descrip-tion of internalisation in the development of thinking suggests that the process is more complex than this question posed by sociocultural theo-rists allows:

> An *interpersonal process is transformed into an intrapersonal one*. Every function in the child's cultural development appears twice: first, on the social level, and later, on the individual level; first, *between people* (*interpsychological*), and then *inside* the child (*intrapsy-chological*). This applies equally to voluntary attention, to logical memory, and to the formation of concepts.
>
> (Vygotsky, 1978 p. 57)

The two schools do, however, have this in common: *they both emphasise the crucial role of activity in learning, not just physical activity but thinking, talking, listening and watching as well as doing.*

Research also indicates that good learners tend to have what are called good metacognitive strategies (Bruner, 1996). Metacognition is a general term which refers to a second-order form of thinking: think-ing about thinking. It includes a variety of self-awareness processes to help plan, monitor, orchestrate and control one's own learning. Such learners monitor their learning using strategies like self-questioning, in order to get the purpose of learning clear, searching for connections and conflicts with what is already known, and judging whether their understanding of the material is sufficient. *An essential aspect of metacog-nition is that learners monitor or regulate their own learning*, and here self-assessment and self-evaluation are crucial.

Self-assessment has rather a bad press since it can be caricatured as children giving themselves marks for their own work. But what is meant here (and self-evaluation is probably the better term) is much more a process of evaluating, with guidance from the teacher, how well a piece of work meets the teacher's requirement or whether it is an improve-ment on a previous piece of work. As we outlined above: the learner has to reflect on her performance in relation to the standard expected and how it can improve. But pupils need help with this: they need to be taught how to do it. It is part of the process of encouraging pupils to take responsibilty for their learning, to 'own' it, and this involves being able to make their own evaluations, rather than being completely dependent on the teacher to tell them how good or weak a piece of work is.

One could be forgiven for thinking that this wide range of views and theories on learning is not particularly helpful to the teacher, or the teacher educator. However, research carried out during 1995 and 1996 on effective teachers of literacy and numeracy by the Universities of Exeter and Plymouth, and King's College London on behalf of the Teacher Training Agency (TTA) have some pertinent findings, both for this book and for what we can usefully take from learning theory. The numeracy study (Askew, Brown, Rhodes, Johnson and Wiliam, 1997) found that the most effective teachers of numeracy in young children had a 'connectionist' as opposed to a transmission or discovery teaching orientation. That is, these teachers believed in the value of getting children to think and talk about what they were learning, and to make connections among different areas of mathematics and different ideas in the same area of mathematics. Similarly, the effective teachers of literacy (Medwell, Wray, Poulson and Fox, 1998) placed a high priority on meaning and on making connections: between word, sentence and text, and between reading and writing.

What we can take from this research which resonates with much of the work on learning theory is the emphasis on thinking and meaning-making. This supports the view that learning is an active process, so the learner must be encouraged to think about what they are learning, to make sense of it, and to link it with other concepts, constructs or pieces of information. To this we can add that the learner needs to be made aware of their own learning and its progress, which again is an active process. Finally, other research indicates that the social setting of learning and the interactions between teacher and pupil, and pupil and pupil, have an important role to play in the learning process.

THE RESEARCH

As we have hinted, the aim of this study was to describe a range of teaching, assessment and feedback practice used in primary classrooms, underpinned by sound approaches to learning. In order to do this we worked with 'expert' teachers of seven-year-olds (Y2) and eleven-year-olds (Y6) over four terms, observing their work, and talking to them about teaching, assessment, feedback and learning. We also spoke to some of the children about learning. We chose Y2 and Y6 teachers because we have found throughout our research that this is a helpful way of illuminating key differences between infant and junior school practice. In Y6 we focused on the teaching of English, mathematics and science, in Y2 on the teaching of reading, writing and mathematics.

The research study was carried out in two local education authorities (LEAs). These are quite different from each other in size and type: one is a large home county and the other a London borough. Between them (and within) they cover a wide range of catchment areas, from inner city to rural, and size and type of primary schools.

Why did we decide to work with *expert* teachers and how did we choose them? If we had been interested in teaching practice in general we would have carried out a survey or worked with a random sample. However, since the aim of the project was to describe the practice of *good* primary teachers, the best thing was to focus on *good* teachers. Of course, the definition of a good teacher is not straightforward. We decided to use the term 'expert teacher' in setting up the research since it is easier to identify individuals who are operating at the extremes of any range. The criteria used to select the teachers were agreed on the basis of discussion between the research team and the LEAs. The teachers were chosen by the LEA inspector involved and the head of the school; thus there was some consensus about both the criteria used and the individuals chosen (see Appendix).

We worked with six Y2 teachers and six Y6 teachers in each of the two LEAs – twenty-four teachers in all. They covered a wide age range and years of experience in teaching, although only two were men. There were 20 schools involved in suburban, town, inner city and rural settings taking children from a broad range of family backgrounds.

Once the 20 schools were identified, we visited them in June 1997 to interview the headteachers to get a general picture of the school, policy and practice on curriculum, teaching and assessment and to meet with the teachers selected. The fieldwork was based on observation and interview, but we also used two new techniques: the Quote Sort and the Four Card Activity. The Four Card Activity involved teachers in a discussion about theories of learning. Four individual statements about four theories of learning were presented on separate cards one at a time and teachers were invited to agree or disagree with the theories. When teachers agreed with theories they were asked about the implications for teaching. The Quote Sort involved teachers in sorting 14 quotes (taken from teachers' earlier interviews) into Agree, Partially Agree and Disagree categories. The quotes focused on teaching, assessment and feedback strategies and on pupil learning. After sorting, teachers were invited to discuss the reasons for their choices[4] and probed on the implications for learning.

Over the course of the project we worked with 24 teachers in 20 schools (reducing to 22 in 19 schools as one teacher left and one became ill) and for a term involved 10 teachers in more detailed study. During this time we carried out 90 interviews (20 headteacher interviews, 70 teacher interviews), 108 lesson observations, 23 Four Card activities, 22 Quote Sorts. Interviews, observations, Four Card and Quote Sort activity data for the case study teachers were merged and analysed using NUDIST (a computer programme for analysing text). The information from the other teachers was analysed by hand using standard techniques of comparison and analysis. This was used to augment the NUDIST analysis. A quantitative cluster analysis was also carried out for the Quote Sort data for all teachers. The various analyses were integrated and themes developed. Finally, our preliminary findings were discussed with the teachers in two focus group interviews.

In the next chapter we will describe the range of lesson patterns we observed; this will provide the context for the more thematic analyses of teaching, assessment and feedback in subsequent chapters.

Notes

1 *Teaching, Assessment and Feedback Strategies: Expert Primary Practice (TAFS)*, ESRC, Ref R000237096
2 *National Assessment in Primary Schools: An Evaluation. Phases 1 and 2 (NAPS 1 and 2)*, ESRC, Ref R000232192 and R000234438
3 *Teacher Feedback to Young Children in Formative Assessment*, ESRC, Ref R00023378
4 Detailed information about both these techniques can be obtained from the authors.

Chapter 2

Lesson patterns

INTRODUCTION

As part of the thrust towards raising standards in literacy and numeracy, there are now precise guidelines on the length and content of these lessons, the ways in which pupils should be grouped, the teaching strategies to be used and how time should be divided among different activities. In the Literacy Hour the required lesson structure is shown as a four-stage format represented diagrammatically by a clock divided into four parts (see Figure 2.1) outlining how much time should be devoted to particular teacher and pupil activities and how many children

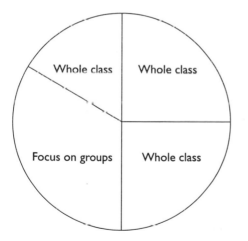

Figure 2.1 Teacher's audiences during the Literacy Hour
The circle represents a one-hour lesson. The subdivisions show the teacher's audience during those sections of time. (Source, DfEE, 1998)

should be involved at each stage. Although shown as four activities, the form the lesson takes is one of teacher input, pupil activities and teacher feedback.

The Numeracy Lesson is shown as a three-stage format (Clear Start – Main Teaching and Pupil Activities – Plenary) represented in a table (see Table 2.1) and once again prescribing the time devoted to each stage, the size of pupil group and the types of task for teacher and pupil.

Overall, in the teaching of both literacy and numeracy, there is clear guidance to use whole-class teaching and 'focused' teaching (working intensively with one or two groups once the children are set to task). There is a requirement to provide one hour for literacy and from between 45 minutes to 60 minutes for numeracy per day, leaving some freedom about the structure of other lessons.

These prescribed structures were just beginning to hit schools when we were working with our expert teachers. Clearly they had been designing lessons and using different formats for a long time, so, what were the lesson patterns *they* used? Were they similar to those proposed for literacy and numeracy? Did they repeatedly use the same lesson pattern or did they vary their repertoire?

Table 2.1 A typical 45–60 minute numeracy lesson (Years 1–6)

5–10 minutes Clear start	Whole class	Oral work and mental calculation to rehearse, sharpen and develop skills
30–40 minutes Main teaching and pupil activities	Whole class or groups or pairs or as individuals	Main teaching input and pupil activities
10–15 minutes Plenary	Whole class	Plenary to round off lesson, sort out misconceptions, summarise key facts, link to other work

HOW DID THE TEACHERS STRUCTURE LESSON TIME?

We observed 89 full lessons and one of the things we were struck by was the variety of lesson shapes or patterns in use. Our teachers varied the ways in which they divided up lesson time and in the size of group they focused on. We were able to identify six different lesson patterns:

1   The three-stage format version 1;
2   The three-stage format version 2;
3   A beginning, a middle and a parting statement format;
4   The one-stage format – commanding the attention of a whole group for a whole lesson;
5   The multistage format – working with whole class on short bursts of different activities;
6   Working with individuals for short amounts of time across whole lesson.

The six patterns are described in more detail in the following sections, together with some illustrations of the patterns in use in different lessons.

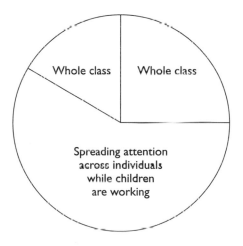

Figure 2.2 Lesson format – Pattern 1

Pattern 1: Three-stage format version 1 (Figure 2.2)

In this lesson pattern, the teacher divided her time into three parts involving:

*   teacher commanding attention of whole class and giving input;
*   children working on activity/activities while teacher tours the room, interacting with individuals, addressing groups or the whole class

at times – generally spreading her attention across the class members;

- teacher commanding attention of the whole class and giving input.

In this arrangement, time was allocated clearly to each part. Introductions varied in length as did middle sections when the children were doing activities, but the teacher always left time to make an input at the end of the lesson and this involved feedback about what children had achieved or a summary of what they had been learning.

The following is an example of Pattern 1 in action.

Maths lesson on addition

In this lesson, a class of 25 Y2 children were practising adding, something they had already been taught. One classroom assistant was present who listened carefully to the teacher's introduction and had been clearly briefed on what the teacher expected her to do.

Teacher's introduction – whole class on carpet   5 minutes

All the children were sitting on the carpet around the teacher's chair. She held up two different maths worksheets on addition and said 'Look at these! They may look easy like this one, 5 + 4, but some are difficult, like 24 + 18'. Using humour, she repeated 'Difficult! Mmm Hmm!!' She explained that everyone would be given one of these and they would have to work down the list of sums. She read out some of the sums on each sheet and drew their attention to the bottom of the harder sheet where it said that if they had finished they were to add a ten to all the answers. The teacher sent out a group of eight children to work with the assistant; she gave out the differentiated worksheets naming the children one by one and off they went to their tables. The children were very lively and the teacher monitored behaviour throughout the introduction by reprimanding named children in a quiet, firm way.

Spreading attention   45 minutes

When the children had settled to the task, the teacher spread her attention across the class and took time to visit every child (except those working with the assistant). The techniques she used during this period were: asking children with wrong answers to explain how they did the sum; listening to explanations and having brief discussions, often re-explaining how to find answers; asking children to show her how they were using fingers to 'count on'; asking children to demonstrate how they were using cubes to count; asking children to identify patterns or showing children patterns in the adding (e.g. $3 + 4 = 7$ and $13 + 4 = 17$); redirecting children to use cubes when they were finding difficulty with mental addition; demonstrating the use of 10 blocks and single cubes; reminding children to start with the larger number first before counting on. When individuals had finished the sheets and brought them up to her, she marked them while asking the children to answer each sum and then ticking correct answers or getting them to re-think wrong answers. On the back of some sheets she wrote assessment comments while reading them to the child: 'Kim completed all these sums independently. She used cubes to help her and is getting to know her number bonds to 10'.

This part of the lesson was peppered with evaluative feedback to the whole class about how well they were working.

Drawing the class together – whole class on carpet   *10 minutes*

The children gathered in front of the teacher on the carpet. She wrote on a flip chart $3 + 2$ and $13 + 2$ and revised the fact that both answers ended in 5 (5 and 15) and that the difference was 10 – indicating the ten in 13 and 15. She repeated this idea with three more examples. She invited the children to contribute: 'Who can give me a one-digit number?' and used children's explanations as part of this short session. If children gave wrong answers, she simply repeated the question with emphasis until the correct answer was given.

Although the pattern was observed in lessons covering a wide range of topics, (and was the most popular pattern overall) it was used often for writing (poetry, story writing, factual writing, formation of letters, and work at sentence and word level). Most commonly however, the teachers used this pattern in maths lessons (on the four number operations, graph making, probability, shape and open-ended investigative work). Drawing children together at the end was a very important component of maths lessons when the teachers took the opportunity to drive home key learning points.

Pattern 2: Three-stage format version 2 (Figure 2.3)

This lesson pattern also made use of three stages but differed from the one described above through the teacher's actions in the middle stage while the children were engaged in activities. Once again, teachers devoted

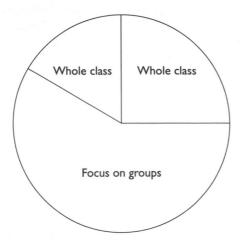

Figure 2.3 Lesson format – Pattern 2

an amount of time to drawing the class together at the end to give a summary of what had been 'learned', often asking for examples from children in turn and in each working group. The pattern looked like this:

- teacher commanding attention of whole class and giving input;
- teacher *focusing her attention on one group*, with minimal interaction with rest of the class;
- teacher commanding attention of whole class, giving input and often asking for contributions from members of the class.

Some teachers using this pattern had other adults working in the classroom – special needs support staff, classroom assistants, students, parents – to whom groups of children were assigned. Other teachers had no extra support but allowed children who were not in focus groups to work independently, at times scanning the room to keep a check on progress or making a 'whip round' tour. Once again, this pattern was observed in lessons covering a range of topics: forces and energy in Y6 science, poetry writing, reading comprehension, the four number operations, data interpretation and opportunities for children to use and apply maths in open-ended investigative work. An example follows of pattern 2 in action.

Writing lesson

In this lesson, a class of 30 Y2 children were writing stories. One classroom assistant was present and she worked with two children who found writing difficult. From assessment of their work, the teacher had identified a group who needed reminding about the structure of sentences. She organised the class so that she could focus her attention on that group.

Teacher's introduction   *15 minutes*

The teacher gathered all the children in front of her on the carpet and announced 'Today we are going to write a story about a strange noise'. Using dramatic voice techniques she said 'If I SHOUT you know what that sound is. If I whisper you know what that sound is . . . if the bell goes at lunch time you know what that sound is . . .'. 'But supposing you were somewhere – in the house, in a park, at school . . . you heard a noise but you couldn't tell what it was . . . It might be really quiet or it might be really loud . . .'. She told the children to close their eyes and think of the answers to these questions: quiet or loud, one little noise or one that carries on? She explained that the noise is strange – one that they can't identify at the beginning of the story.

To help them to make some initial decisions, she chose several children and asked each one the same simple open questions: 'Will your noise be quiet or loud?'; 'where will you be when you hear the noise?'. To the whole class she explained 'You can decide on anything at all: day or night; something ordinary or something strange'.

The teacher asked for words that might mean 'strange' and accepted a few plausible suggestions. She asked, 'Is there a word beginning with "w"?' No-one knew and at that point she rolled down the whiteboard and revealed a list of adjectives, including 'weird' – to which she drew the children's attention. She explained to the children that she had put together a selection of 'noise words' that they might want to use. The children spontaneously chanted down the list. The teacher explained that she had also written up 'some beginnings' which they could use such as 'One morning I . . .' or 'As I lay in bed . . .' and a few others. She asked for volunteers to complete each of the sentences and repeated each child's response slowly while looking around at the rest of the class and nodding, thus affirming that they were perfectly acceptable. The rest of the story was left up to the children, the instructions being to explain how the sound was eventually detected and what it turned out to be.

Before the children began to write their stories, the teacher reminded them to look in their writing books to see if they had been left a message. She was referring here to written feedback she had put in their books. Sometimes there would be instructions to practise writing and spelling particular words, sometimes there would be a commendation or a question relating directly to what a child had written, such as '*I wonder what would have happened if you had gone into the cave?*'. At times children would answer questions like this and enter into a written dialogue with the teacher.

To sum up her introduction, the teacher explained today's context: '*This is a best guess day – nobody is coming to me for words. Try sounding out your words, listen to your words, think back to what we did in our sound work and have a go at spelling*'. She sent the children to their different groups and joined her focus group of eight children.

Focus group teaching   35 minutes

When the group of eight children had written the date on their page, the teacher announced '*Today we will focus on sentences*'. She quizzed: '*What is a sentence? A sentence has got to make . . .*'. A girl finished the sentence with '*sense*' and the teacher approved. She continued with a set of questions: '*How would you know it was a sentence? What comes at the beginning?*'. Children chanted '*capital letter*' and the teacher agreed and asked what came at the end of a sentence. The teacher gave examples of sentences and unfinished sentences. She told the children '*Tell me if this is a sentence . . . I was going to. . . .*' The children chorused '*No*'. Then, '*I made some cheese rolls*'. Children answered '*Yes*'. She elicited from children that a sentence has to make sense and be finished.

Her instructions to the children were '*Think of what you are going to say. Make sure it's a sentence – make sure it makes sense and is finished. When you are sure it is finished, write a full stop*'. These instructions were repeated twice more. She explained that she would come round to read their sentences and when she saw a proper sentence, she would allow them to put a counter at the end of it.

Individual teaching of focus group children   30 minutes

The teacher then gave individual attention to each child in the group, standing behind them and leaning over their work. Her purpose was to reinforce what she had taught about sentence making. Sometimes she asked questions to prompt recall of the punctuation involved ('*Is that your name? Are you important? So what does your name need?*'). Sometimes she asked '*What's wrong with this?*' (pointing to a space where a full stop should be). At other times she asked a child to read her '*the whole sentence'* and quizzed them about whether it made sense or if it was finished. Often this was repeated many times till the child cottoned on. For spelling she stuck to her guns and did not give spellings automatically. Rather, children were told to say the initial sound, look this up in their own word books and check words already there to see if they could find the word they were after. Often she helped individuals to break down components in words. Sometimes she directed children's attention back to the prompt list of words on the whiteboard and got them to identify as far as possible the word they were after. To move children on she would say, *'Tell me what you are going to write next? Fine. Now write that'.* Feedback consisted of praise for writing a sentence and using capitals and full stops. When a child completed a proper sentence the teacher placed a counter on the full stop (a kind of tangible reward).

Several minutes before the end of the session, the teacher called the attention of the rest of the class with *'Remember, a good story needs a good ending – bring your story to an end now.'* She left the focus group at this point and circulated round the others, working with several individuals. The class had been working well during her time with the focus group. Just before playtime, she returned to the focus group and asked one or two by name to count how many correct sentences they had managed to write (indicated by the number of counters they had been awarded.)

Debriefing the whole class   *20 minutes*

After playtime the teacher talked to the whole class who were sitting on the carpet in front of her. She asked individuals to come out front and read out their stories (four girls and three boys). They were of differing abilities but they all received a general pat on the back. While they were reading out their stories, the teacher was making assessment notes on their 'speaking and listening' skills.

Overall, pattern 2 was used more by Y2 than Y6 teachers. However, teachers of both age groups used this pattern during lessons on number, sentence level work and reading comprehension.

Pattern 3: A beginning, a middle and a parting statement (Figure 2.4)

On a number of occasions we observed lessons with two clear stages to which the bulk of time was devoted but with a less shaped ending than

Parting statement to whole class

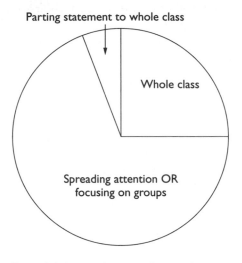

Figure 2.4 Lesson format – Pattern 3

the two patterns already described i.e. the teacher gave only a parting statement at the end of the lesson which was either an evaluative feedback comment about how well the lesson had gone – '*Right, well done*', a command to tidy up, or simply an instruction about routines. – '*Get ready for lunch*' or '*Put your work in the finished work tray*'. This pattern occurred mainly in English lessons (handwriting, writing, word level work, reading comprehension) and rarely in maths and science.

Two teachers explained honestly that although they intended to have a plenary session at the end of most lessons, they often ran out of time. However, there were other reasons why teachers did not set aside time to address the whole class at the end of these lessons.

In the case of writing, some teachers did not draw the class together at the end because everyone was at a different stage with their work, general feedback seemed irrelevant and writing was likely to continue into other lesson time. Also, teachers omitted a plenary when an activity was something routinely done by children individually when they came in the mornings (e.g. practise handwriting) or routinely done as a run up to assembly (e.g. 10 minutes phonics practise). The pattern also occurred during sessions when children were working on many different subject activities, very different worksheets in the same subject (such as reading comprehension or maths) or when Y6 teachers taught a 'set' or ability group, took away exercise books to mark and gave feedback on the work at the beginning of the next session with that set (maths, English).

Pattern 4: One-stage format

There were times when our teachers controlled a whole lesson, when they did not set a task and tour the room but stayed in one place keeping the children with them for the whole session. Teachers used this pattern when there was something they wanted a whole group of children to learn. For example, a Y2 teacher read two stories to a whole class and helped them to identify two very different story structures, while a Y6 teacher used a single text with the whole class to introduce them to the ideas of inference and deduction.

In a Y6 science lesson to the whole class, detailed at the beginning of the book, the teacher gave a clear explanation and demonstration of how to record scientific findings on charts, a technique they would need in much of their work. A Y2 arithmetic lesson involved a game where children all facing the teacher were invited to ask questions to find a mystery number (e.g. *'Is it less than 70?' 'Is it an even number?'* – if the teacher answered yes to both of these, she would remove all numbers that could be eliminated from a grid from 0–100. In the group situation, children were able to learn from other children's questions.

Importantly, lessons of this pattern lasted no more than 30 minutes and all involved the teacher in inviting contributions from the children in different ways: getting them to read aloud one at a time, saying a chorus in unison, inviting guesses (maths) or inviting children to recall previous knowledge (science). This pattern most closely represents traditional whole-class teaching; although the level of interaction varied, it was generally low and depended upon children being willing to volunteer answers. This pattern also provided a useful organisational technique for 'oral testing', when teachers fired spot mental arithmetic questions to each individual in a group.

Pattern 5: Multi-stage format (Figure 2.5)

A fifth pattern was discernible when Y6 teachers divided up English and science lessons into 10–15 minute chunks, working with the whole class and using a variety of techniques. They alternated their own input with getting children to do something and gave short bursts of time to each, sometimes sticking to a timed plan. Short bursts of time were given to these techniques:

- children brainstorming;
- children reading out examples;
- teacher relaying knowledge and facts;
- teacher reading aloud;
- teacher demonstrating;
- teacher inviting children's contributions through question and answer;
- children doing short, active tasks alone or in pairs;
- children coming out front and demonstrating;
- teacher asking for one answer from each child in Round Robin fashion.

Here we see this format being applied to a science lesson.

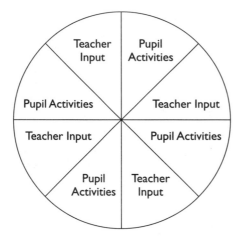

Figure 2.5 Multi-stage lesson format – Pattern 5

Science

The Y6 teacher asks a number of questions about what it means to be 'fit'. She invites Stephen to run on the spot for three minutes and demonstrates how his heart rate increases; by taking his pulse she measures his heart rate before and afterwards. The teacher leads a question and answer session on heart rate to find out what children know. Based on this she gives extra facts about the heart, circulation, and raising heart rate through exercise. The children in pairs are invited to test their own heart rate before and after exercise. They do step-ups on chairs while the teacher sets a certain amount of time, using a stop watch, and then they measure and record heart rates. The teacher asks different children to report their heart rates and where there are differences, she invites comparisons and reasoning. After two more sets of increasingly strenuous exercise, the same questioning is used to provoke thinking.

This type of multi-stage, multi-technique lesson was observed only in Y6 classes. It can be described as 'interactive whole-class teaching' and is clearly different from the traditional version described in (4) above.

Pattern 6: Working with individuals for short amounts of time (Figure 2.6)

Sometimes our teachers divided their lesson time into approximately 10-minute bursts when they gave their attention to individual children. We observed this in reading and maths. In Y2, teachers spent time hearing individuals read, not as part of a focus group, but withdrawn from the classroom. Nearly always this interaction involved some assessment (where the teacher gauged the level of a child's performance and recorded something about it).

In one Y6 classroom, the entire lesson involved the teacher in monitoring children's reading diaries: each diary contained a record of the books the child had read, together with the child's critique or review of those books and comments about the child's own reading progress. Once again this was an assessment activity but of a slightly different

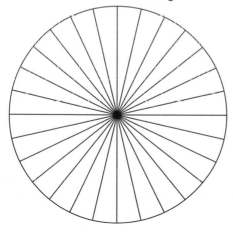

Individual conferencing

Figure 2.6 Lesson format – Pattern 6

nature – the child had engaged in self-assessment and the teacher and child had negotiated the way forward. In other Y6 classrooms, when children were working on individual maths cards at different levels as part of a whole school scheme, teachers spent bursts of time questioning and helping individuals and once again this involved assessment in the form of checking and correcting work, but also working out why a child was going wrong. The following is an example of such a maths lesson.

Maths lesson

A class of 30 Y6 children were working individually on cards dealing with a wide range of mathematical topics.

Teacher's introduction   *2 minutes*

'*Take out your maths exercise books*' instructed the teacher. '*Remember we are aiming to complete 3 cards per week. You have time to complete a whole card in this next hour. Aim today to do a whole card if not more*'. (At this point the teacher organised some children into pairs to play maths games arising out of their work.) She also gave instructions to four boys whose names were on the board – Adam, Bill, Dod and Tim. '*You have a few corrections*'; '*I need to talk to you*'.

Working with individuals   *57 minutes*

Case One: Adam
The teacher had marked Adam's test and he had got some wrong. In relation to this, she had written out the following explanations:

Metres to centimetres	Centimetres to metres
3.25m = 325cm	129cms = 1.29m
1.45m = 145cm	450cms = 4.50m

Her instructions were: '*Correct Card 37, 1a) 1d) 2a) 2b)*'.

She sat alongside Adam and took him through the wrong answers. Some techniques used were: getting Adam to read out the question;

asking how he had carried out the sums; explaining what he had done incorrectly; suggesting another way of doing the sums; recalling previous work to prompt thinking; asking him to predict. 'Will your answer be in motion or centimetres?'; demonstrating how to do the sums using plenty of examples.

Adam was clearly learning from all this – he responded 'All right. Yes! I get it'.

Case Two: Bill

As with Adam, Bill had got some things wrong in his test of equivalent fractions. The teacher had marked the work, seen where the error lay and had written out some fractions in his book and it was through these examples that she did her teaching.

She asked Bill if he had used a calculator to do the sums. No, he hadn't so he was sent to get a calculator.

The question he had got wrong was 'Is 6 eighths the same as 8 tenths?' The teacher explained what she had written in his book. 'You must remember that 6 eighths really means 6 divided by 8; 8 tenths means 8 divided by ten.' She had written loads more fractions down and instructed him to read each one, explaining to her what they really meant. 'Three quarters means 3 divided by 4; seven eighths means 7 divided by 8,' said Bill. The teacher praised him as he went through several examples. Coming back to the original problem, she asked him to show her how he would calculate 6 divided by 8 using the calculator. He could do this. She asked him to read the answer and showed him that he needed to record the answer. She explained that he would now have to see what 8 tenths came out as (and he managed this). She focused his attention on the two decimal answers and asked 'Well, are they the same?'. Bill answered 'No' and the teacher said 'Well write "No" '. She reinforced this process by using another example but letting Bill talk her through the steps. She ended the session with 'Can you tell the answer to these by just looking?'. He answered 'No' and the teacher left him with 'No. So you have to do it that way'.

Case Three: Dod

Dod came up to the teacher and said he was stuck with '*Put these angles in order of size*'.

Several angles were displayed on Dod's work card. The teacher pointed to one of them – '*Is that a right angle?*' she queried. He wasn't sure. '*Want to test it with your square corner?*'. She supervised how he placed the square corner on to the angle, '*Put it on exactly*'. Then asked '*Is it larger or smaller than a right angle?*' Dod answered correctly ('smaller'). The same process was repeated with two other angles. '*Are your answers in the correct order?*' queried the teacher. 'No' said Dod. The teacher advised, '*Well sometimes you need to test – you can't rely on your eyes*'.

Case Four: Tim

Tim came up to the teacher. He was doing his corrections and wanted to check about adding angles of a triangle. He had been using a protractor but had got some answers wrong. The teacher asked him to show her how he was using the protractor. She stood back and observed him using the instrument. (Correctly). On a new example she set him, he measured the three angles accurately and wrote in the three sizes. She asked him to add the three sizes and they came to 180°. She asked him to identify the different types of triangle he had there ('scalene' 'isosceles' 'equilateral' – he knew them all). She reinforced: '*So if I take any triangle, "scalene", "isosceles", "equilateral" – what will the three angles add to?*'. Tim knew. It was 180°. She added a challenge – '*How many degrees in a straight angle?*' and gave a clue by making a model with a ruler and a pencil'. '180 degrees' said Tim. She left him with '*Brilliant*'.

In between these case studies, the teacher answered innumerable queries, demonstrated the accurate use of compasses, showed two children how to play a maths game, partnered people up, supervised the work of the helper with one less able girl. It was a massive management exercise.

End of lesson   *a few seconds*

The teacher told all the children to finish the sum they were on. It was time to stop for lunch.

THE POPULARITY AND USE OF DIFFERENT PATTERNS

Of these six patterns, the most popular was the three-stage format version 1, when teachers gave an introduction, set the children to activities and circulated, spreading their attention across the class before drawing the whole class together at the end for some kind of feedback. Two patterns were used much more rarely: keeping the whole class together for 30-minute stints under full control of the teacher with no desk activities, and the more dynamic multi-stage, multi-activity, whole-class lessons.

Y2 and Y6 teachers differed in their use of lesson patterns more than they coincided: more Y2 teachers favoured the use of focusing on one group in the three-stage format, while it was only Y6 teachers who were observed to use the multi-stage, multi-activity lesson pattern. Some teachers were systematic about certain types of pattern and repeated these regularly, regardless of subject taught: at least five favoured focus group teaching in the middle part of lessons while another six repeatedly spread their attention across the class at this time. One (Y2) teacher used the same focus group pattern in every single one of the five lessons we observed her teach. Two Y6 teachers used the multi-stage, multi-activity format more than anything else while 10 teachers (seven Y2 and three Y6) used a variety of the six lesson patterns identified.

WHAT CAN WE LEARN FROM THE TEACHERS' CHOICE OF PATTERN?

These expert teachers, besides intuitively using structures which were later to be recommended for teaching literacy and numeracy, regularly used a range of other successful patterns. Some teachers chose formats that '*worked for them*', while others explored different formats for different types of lesson. Clearly if there is something that everyone needs to know, it is expedient to involve the whole class; if there is a need to motivate children, many short interesting tasks and activities are required (including, as the children later told us, a practical hands-on element) and these need to be orchestrated by the teacher. Where children are taking time to finish something, such as a piece of writing, there may be no need for a plenary. Where basic skills of number or writing are being practised there is a constant need for reminding and consolidation through the use of focused teaching and plenaries.

ORGANISATIONAL STRATEGIES

Teaching involves planning and managing pupil groups; the expert teachers that we worked with did not always manage or organise things in exactly the same ways.

In our observations the ways in which classrooms were arranged tended to add to the smooth running of the lessons, especially when resources were easily accessible, there was space between tables, there were quiet corners for quiet work and any whiteboards, blackboards or flip charts were within good view of the group the teacher was addressing.

In all but one instance rooms remained set in the same configuration for the entirety of our research – teachers were comfortable with their arrangements. However, one particularly interesting teacher had intro-duced the norm of changing the layout to suit the type of lesson. For example, when the lesson involved a whole class 30-minute session, desks and chairs were arranged in a horseshoe facing the board; when there were investigations and experiments to be carried out, children themselves moved their desks into blocks to facilitate group work; when it came to a plenary session ('*So let's talk about what we have learned*') children quickly arranged their chairs in a circle with no desks in front. The size of the classes in our study varied between 24 and 32 children with 26 and 28 being the norm. The teachers, as with other aspects of their repertoire, used a variety of ways of grouping children:

- as a whole class;
- in ability 'sets';
- in ability groups;
- in mixed ability groups;
- in pairs; and
- withdrawing an individual from groups.

The use of these groupings was idiosyncratic from teacher to teacher but there were some common practices which point to best match of pupil grouping to the task in hand. Grouping children as a whole class at the beginning and end of lessons was a common organisational strategy of both Y2 and Y6 teachers and one through which they could tell children what was going to happen and what was expected. Teachers of both age groups favoured grouping children as a whole class for teaching the basic skills in English and maths.

Many of the Y6 teachers were in favour of ability setting for maths, with few seeing it as a fitting grouping for English. Ability setting was felt to be appropriate because it was a way of raising standards by doing more class teaching of a group with similar abilities. There was much less evidence of ability setting in infant schools or departments, although two Y2 teachers worked with sets for reading. Teaching reading in ability groups within a class was a fairly common strategy. In writing, more teachers preferred to teach the basic writing skills of punctuation and grammar to ability groups than to the whole class, whereas more preferred to teach 'style and presentation' to the whole class than to ability groups. Ability grouping for maths was strongly supported by teachers and was found to be common in both age groups.

Overall, grouping children by ability was used to allow children to practise something already taught, giving the teacher an opportunity to engage in reinforcement or assessment activities while children were at work. This type of grouping was used to advantage by some teachers to create a context within which they could devote their attention to one group while others worked independently or with a helper.

Mixed ability grouping was used by teachers of both age groups. The most popular context for mixed ability grouping was practical and/or open-ended investigative work in science. Pairing was used in a similar way. Often teachers matched pairs who would work well together and at other times allowed children to work in friendship pairs. Mixed ability grouping and pairing appeared to be selected so that children could learn from others in a socially interactive way.

Withdrawing individuals from other groups was a strategy used by teachers of both age groups, mainly to look at individual progress in reading, and so as a kind of assessment.

Overall there was strong agreement between Y2 and Y6 teachers over the use of pupil groupings. Teachers appear to have selected groupings for the purpose of either teaching, learning or assessment. Mixed ability grouping, pairing and pupil-chosen groups were for 'finding out' and collaborative tasks and were used to encourage talk as a means of learning. In contrast, whole-class grouping and ability grouping were strategies used more for relaying knowledge (direct teaching). Ability sets and ability groups were convenient for consolidation of learning at a pupil's own level. Withdrawing individuals from groups was a means of assessing progress.

The lesson patterns described and illustrated above, and the organisational strategies, form the context against which the more detailed teaching, assessment and feedback strategies are set. We now move, first, to the teaching strategies.

Chapter 3

Teaching strategies

INTRODUCTION

The 23 expert teachers were using a wide range of teaching strategies and they selected them at particular times for particular reasons, drawing on the repertoire they had in store. By definition, repertoire means 'the entire stock of things available in a field or of a kind'. It would probably be untrue to say we could describe the entire stock of teaching strategies used by the teachers in our study, given that we were not living alongside them in their classrooms day after day. However, based on our visits to them over an 18-month period, we can describe in detail many of the techniques and devices they used to convey knowledge and promote learning in young children.

We wanted to isolate exactly what teachers meant by a 'teaching' strategy as opposed to an 'assessment' strategy or a 'feedback' strategy. And so, bringing together our observations of lessons and the teachers' views, we developed a definition of teaching as

a presentation in various ways of adult-decided knowledge,
skills and understandings.

THE TEACHING STRATEGIES USED BY EXPERT TEACHERS

Teaching involves passing on (and reinforcing) knowledge, skills and understanding and we identified three types of teaching strategy: **informing, reinforcing and supporting learning**. We were able to unpack and give names to the techniques our teachers were using in each of those categories and these are explained in the following sections.

I Informing

Informing means just that. We found seven strategies that teachers used in passing on information to their classes:

- Relaying knowledge;
- Explaining;
- Instructing;
- Relaying ways of learning;
- Modelling;
- Demonstrating; and
- Conveying examples of children's work.

a) Relaying knowledge

Perhaps the most common of the informing strategies was relaying knowledge. That strategy involved teachers in broadcasting or transmitting facts and information: factual information arising in all the core and foundation subjects; meanings and definitions; tricks; tips; memory jogs and snippets of general knowledge (often added as extra facts to children's own answers or contributions).

The function of relaying knowledge was just that – to tell children things that the teacher felt they needed to know. However, in teachers' views there were two important caveats. First, children did not always retain facts or knowledge which was too far removed from their everyday experience. A Y2 teacher in a Home Counties school reported:

> I told them all this information about India – and they had to go off and write about it. It was so far removed from anything [they knew] – it didn't go well.

Second, there were dangers associated with too much transmission: delivering a monologue did not ensure that children were listening and children would not learn if the teacher talked for too long and did not get the children involved quickly enough in doing something. (Certainly, in our lesson observations there were no long periods of the teacher just 'holding forth').

As the following extract from a lesson transcript shows, our teachers generally preferred an interactive approach to relaying knowledge and transmitting facts, choosing to weave in their own input with

contributions from children and then building upon these contributions to give further explanation.

Teacher: Can anybody tell me anything about how we go about writing poems?

Calvin: The lines have to be short.

Teacher: Right, so we have to use short lines. They don't always have
to be but we talked about making them short because that
way we can be concise and we can use language in a creative way.

Kemal: Every line begins with a capital letter.

Teacher: Good. Every line begins with a capital letter.

Tess. It's about feelings.

Teacher: OK. It's a vehicle, poetry is a vehicle for feelings. What is it
about the way we write poetry, about the way we can struc-
ture the actual words we put together that is different from
writing a story?

Harry: Making something seem like something else.

Teacher: OK, and what's that word, can you remember what we call
that?

Leah: Analogy.

Teacher: Analogy – likening something to something else – the snow
fell softly, like feathers. That's an analogy. Now what else?

Charlie: Simile.

Teacher: Simile is like....

Harry: A saying.

Teacher: Similes are sayings, right, they are set sayings.

Paula: As fat as a pig.

Teacher: Yes, as fat as a pig.

Clova: Doesn't have to be in sentences.

Teacher: That's right, there doesn't have to be (as we use in stories)
proper sentences. You can use lists of words, strings of words,
you can connect them in any way you like because the rules
are much broader – you can use your imagination and really
go to town.

Teachers told us that relaying knowledge was an important part of
teaching all areas of the curriculum and some topics within English,
maths and science could only be learned if children were told about
them directly.

English

Teachers believed that the following elements of English required them to give direct instruction:

- letter formation and joins in cursive writing;
- the punctuation details and layout of speech in writing;
- the rules and patterns in the spelling of words;
- suspense and other elements of style in writing; and
- different figures of speech and their use.

Grammar was another area that teachers felt had to be specifically taught. To quote one of the Y2 teachers:

> *Children need to know grammatical conventions and they are not going to know them unless you tell them – you have to teach the points.*

We observed teachers devoting time to the teaching of grammar. Among the lessons observed were a whole half hour on 'verbs' and tenses in a Y6 class and 20 minutes on 'adjectives' in a Y2 class.

Maths

Following the same argument, there was general agreement about teaching some aspects of maths. To quote a Y6 teacher:

> *If I was teaching percentages or angles there is no other way of doing it than actually passing on my knowledge directly.*

Shape, Space and Measures were other areas mentioned as particularly requiring teacher transmission of facts. In maths lessons, we observed teachers relaying knowledge in the following ways: interpreting questions in textbooks for children and telling them the methods to use; telling children the meanings of words and giving definitions of mathematical terms and ideas (*'Probability is about finding what chance there is of something happening'*); passing on the conventional ways of recording numbers (e.g. how to express a fraction) and giving a running commentary on how a pattern was emerging from a sequence of numbers. (*'Four, five, seven, ten . . . what is happening here is the numbers are going up in a certain pattern. From four to five is one; from five to seven is two; from seven to ten is three . . . so the pattern is one, two, three, four. So to find the next in the series of numbers we need to make a jump of four. Ten jumps by four to 14 . . . and so on').*

Science

In the science lessons we observed, relaying knowledge was a major component of the teacher's repertoire. Among Y6 teachers there was a general belief that science topics about life processes (reproduction, respiration) and physics (forces, energy) needed very specific teaching of facts and appropriate vocabulary.

Relaying knowledge in different lesson contexts

In any classroom there are lessons when new topics are being intro-duced and there are lessons when children are consolidating or practising what they have learned about those topics. In all subjects, relaying knowledge was, de facto, an important strategy in lessons in which the teacher was teaching something for the first time and where they felt the ideas and information would be new to all or most of the children. A Y2 teacher explained that she was likely to make more use of this strategy than of other strategies at this time:

> *It is usually knowledge-based at the beginning of a new topic. If it is something new then my input is probably more and theirs is less, so they are doing more listening.*

Those lessons were more teacher-led with more exposition because teachers wanted to make sure that everyone in the class or group had grasped the concept. One approach was to *'start low, presume they don't understand'.* Another was to *'repeat it, turn it on its head, turn it round – it's up to the teacher to modify her language so that children of all abilities can grasp concepts.'*

In lessons where children were practising or applying something already taught, teachers did relay knowledge in their introductions but to a lesser degree and often the knowledge was pitched at the middle range of ability. Children then went on to do tasks matched more closely to their different ability levels. There was some evidence that teachers used this strategy more when children were arranged in ability groups, particularly in ability sets. A teacher explained:

> *Because they are grouped by ability, I can teach concepts by chalk and talk.*

Teachers relayed knowledge at all stages of a lesson. Quite often at the beginnings of lessons teachers relayed knowledge to the whole class. The facts transmitted usually focused specifically on the topic of the lesson but not always – sometimes teachers threw out additional related facts. For example, in a maths lesson on how to read a scale on a diagram involving sizing a dinosaur, the teacher gave factual (natural history) information about dinosaurs, thus integrating knowledge and bringing different strands of information together for the children.

In the middle of lessons, teachers often stopped the class and gave out information that had arisen from working with individuals. At the end of lessons teachers spelled out the main facts they had wanted children to learn.

Both Y2 and Y6 teachers described this strategy, agreed that it helped children to learn and that it was an important strategy to use at the onset of a new topic. It was a dominant feature of the Y6 science lessons we observed.

b) Explaining

Explaining was a strategy described by all our teachers and it was generally agreed that a lot of teaching consisted of explaining. In meaning, the strategy of explaining was very close to relaying knowledge but here teachers meant that they elaborated or enlarged upon relayed information by describing further examples or illustrations. Teachers described how they spelled out and clarified *'what something means, how something works'*, by rephrasing information, repeating information, or interpreting one child's answer for the rest of the class.

A Y6 teacher described the function of explaining as *'illuminating so that children can better understand'*. In our observations teachers of both age groups appeared to try anything and everything to make things clear for children. Their oral explanations were often accompanied by other teaching strategies such as modelling or demonstrating and by supportive strategies such as using visual props. As one Y2 teacher expressed it, *'I could explain by using resources like pictures to try and make it clear'*. Another Y2 teacher reported using deliberate mistakes because *'children realise they know it by spotting what you have done wrong'*. Teachers used a variety of other strategies to aid their explanations including repeating children's correct answers or good suggestions slowly and clearly, emphasising key words, allowing children to help other children, telling personal anecdotes, repeating things in many different ways, recapping, using drama and mime to good effect.

Explaining was a widespread strategy in all subjects. Explaining was used slightly more often when the lesson involved teaching something new or in a one-to-one context when a child was having particular difficulty. Explaining was least used when children were set investigations in maths or science. We observed its use in many contexts, in all subjects and stages in lessons, when teachers were addressing the whole class and when they were working with individuals. We observed teachers explaining in order to define the meaning of words, make clear the plot of a story, elucidate why something happens (such as why a candle flame goes out when you put a tin without holes over it, but not when you put a tin with holes over it).

In specific instances a Y2 teacher produced a newspaper to explain what a headline was, another Y2 teacher repeated and used a boy's explanation of making the net of a cube to clarify the process to a whole group, two Y6 teachers used errors to make things clear (one used a nonsense maths example and the other gave examples of non-sentences). A Y2 teacher made a task on using maps clearer by personalising it for one child – looking for the child's own address and showing her how to find it. There were instances of teachers involving children in actions to make understandings clearer: a Y6 teacher invited children to rub hands together to get a sense of friction while an infant teacher asked the whole class to stand up and join hands across the room to get a sense of the length of a dinosaur.

Explaining was used when teachers addressed the whole class at the beginning of lessons; it was also used with individuals who either sought help or asked 'why?' in public or private contexts.

There was no difference between the ways in which Y2 and Y6 teachers used explanation. Rather there were some teachers in both age groups who used a greater variety of explanatory techniques than others in the sample.

c) Instructing

All teachers agreed that 'instructing' had something to do with 'telling'. It was a strategy involving giving commands or instructions to children: '*Look at me!*'; '*Do not use a dictionary*'; '*Use line guides for writing*'.

Instructions such as these were invariably brief, precise and to the point and through using them teachers were directing children to the teacher's requirements. To teachers 'instructing' also had another meaning; it meant teaching a correct and non-negotiable way of doing or going about something. One Y2 teacher described it as '*What I am telling you is the way you do it – there is no alternative*'. Other teachers described how the strategy was rigid and prescriptive and was used when '*teaching something where there is no room for manoeuvre*'.

Instructions in the form of commands were given mainly for organisational reasons ('*Sit down at your table when you think you are ready!*') or to specify how a task should be laid out. ('*Put name, date and title*'). The function of instructing was to specify techniques, procedures and rules that were the only ones to be used – a set of rules one should not deviate from. As another Y2 teacher explained: '*This is the way you do it and you do it in steps 1, 2, 3, 4*'. Instructing in this sense was used when teachers felt there was little chance of children picking up something by themselves. Instructing did not involve the children in anything other than giving quick answers to the teachers. It was a strategy used alongside modelling or demonstrating.

Teachers described using instructing when training children in the safe use of equipment and in the following subject contexts:

Maths

Specifying the steps for multiplying and dividing.
Detailing how calculators work (simply saying to the child '*On-button, that side, turn it on – press!*').

English

Stipulating spelling rules, the rules of grammar (particularly the use of different tenses) and the rules of letter formation.

In this extract a Y2 teacher talks through the rules while she demonstrates the correct formation of letters.

Teacher: The capital Q sits with his bottom on the line, the little one needs to have his tail going right down to the red line. What comes after Q?
Children: R
Teacher: Capital R make sure he stands with his head right up to the top and with our little r we start at the top, to bottom, up and back over. None of this lazy way, this flicking over like some of you do.

We observed teachers both 'giving instructions' as commands and 'instructing'. At the beginning of lessons, after the main input of information, teachers would give specific instructions about carrying out the task. For example, in a session on poetry writing a Y6 teacher stipulated what was required as the first step. She instructed '*Chuck out as many words as possible to describe parts of the flower. I'm not looking for phrases, just single words*'. In a Y2 lesson which combined children's speaking and listening with a science investigation of objects and their materials, the teacher organised children in pairs and gave the following instructions: '*Handle and discuss, describe, think and write*'.

In one-to-one reading contexts, examples of Y2 teachers' instructions were '*Look at the picture*'; '*Ignore words that are difficult, read to the end of the sentence and try to guess the word from the context*'; '*Look carefully at each word – look at letter patterns*'; '*Sound it out. Break the word up. Try the first three letters*'. In this way instructions were used to give tips on learning strategies.

One very specific context for giving instructions was when the older children were practising for national tests in English. In order to prepare them for the story writing test, a Y6 teacher limited her class to set timings: 15 minutes planning and 45 minutes writing. She gave instructions: '*This time we are all going to finish. Remember three clear sections – beginning, middle and end. Link the end to the beginning in some way. Check your punctuation is accurate*'. When children asked if they could make up their own title, the teacher said no. She wanted them to get into the habit of working to fixed titles because that is what the test demanded. To put this in context, the teacher was not so authoritarian at other times; the children were keen to do well in these high profile tests and appreciated these instructions as a succinct summary and reminder of a number of weeks' practice.

In lessons where the teacher was 'instructing' they often provided frameworks or guidelines to steer children through the appropriate steps. We observed Y6 teachers giving planning grids for writing and frameworks for planning a fair test in science, a Y2 teacher providing a set of guidelines for using reference books and teachers of both age groups providing lists of words from which children could select to aid their writing.

When it came to 'instructing', in maths, if all children were to do the same worksheet, teachers of both age groups might rehearse the first two or three questions, specifying step-by-step operations for the sums. In the case of different worksheets for different abilities, teachers of both age groups would sometimes keep the whole class together while specifying the task for each group, before children began on their tasks.

'Instructing' (in the sense of teaching specific steps) was prevalent in lessons in which children were learning something new, but on occasion, in maths, teachers of both age groups revised all the steps of number operations before the children were directed to more practise.

Teachers of both age groups described giving instructions and instructing children to do things in particular ways; in our observations, there was no difference in the ways Y2 and Y6 teachers used these strategies. Instructions were given in all subjects, while instructing was used in handwriting at Y2 and science at Y6, and in both year groups for number operations.

d) Relaying ways of learning

During our lesson observations we became aware that teachers were informing children about ways of learning – strategies they could use or ways in which they could behave that would help them learn. In interview, however, few teachers described this and so it may have been a less conscious strategy. Although this strategy appears to have been widely employed by teachers of both age groups, one Y6 teacher was particularly conscious of using it. This teacher's practice was characterised by constant referral to learning strategies and he explained in interview:

> I think fundamentally that children need to know all of the processes of learning and so that's what I am teaching.

Teachers frequently told children that they would learn by listening. Y2 teachers described this as a particularly important message to young children and one had institutionalised a practice of asking for 'listening ears', indicating her own ears as the children indicated theirs. The same teacher used a similar device for getting children to concentrate, asking for 'thinking heads' while indicating her own brain as the children indicated theirs.

'Thinking about and posing questions' was conveyed to children as another activity that would help them learn. To promote this, one Y6 teacher explained that she encouraged a 'learning ethos – seeking knowledge' and she never reprimanded children for asking questions.

Children were also told that 'checking work' was a useful learning strategy and in one of the maths lessons observed a teacher gave children

a whole range of methods for checking answers. For example, he wrote
$34123 \times 10 = 132$ and asked the children:

> *Why is that NOT the right answer? Think about what you'd expect the*
> *answer to look like?* (When a child responded correctly) *Yes! Every*
> *whole number when multiplied by ten has a 0 on the end! So that's one*
> *way of checking this type of answer.* (Returning to the board, he
> wrote $34 + 231 = 376$, saying) *Why does that have to be wrong?*
> (When no-one responded he explained) *because odd and even*
> *always give an odd answer! So that's another fast check.*

'*One of the things I tell children is that real learning happens when you take*
risks', the teacher told us later in interview. The idea that you learn by
taking risks, getting things wrong and finding out why you were wrong,
was a common message transmitted by both Y2 and Y6 teachers.

Teachers told their classes not to be frightened to put their hands up
and have a go and that they would learn by experimenting with hunches,
'*by trying out something you are not sure about*'. This linked to a common
aim to wean children away from constantly asking the teacher for help,
towards taking more responsibility for their learning and becoming
more independent.

Teachers told children they could learn by seeking help from books,
the Internet and classmates but not by merely copying. They told
children to identify and use the particular tricks or memory jogging
techniques that worked best for them.

Relaying learning strategies in different types of lesson

ENGLISH – WRITING

We observed a lesson where Y6 children were analysing the elements
of a good story. The teacher explained that she had asked them to do
some brainstorming in groups because they could learn by listening to
what other people said and mulling it over, and also by thinking about
the contributions they themselves were going to make to the discussion.

In another example (an interactive whole-class session) the teacher
asked children to call up all the little tricks they had learned that
would help them to write a fairly good, technically correct story. The
children recalled some of strategies they had been taught such as: '*Put*
little signs to yourself to remember capitals and full stops'; '*Keep track of the*
time and leave the last five minutes for checking through'.

MATHS

Encouraging children to use a range of previously taught tricks or memory jogging techniques applied particularly in maths teaching.

Teachers informed children that it would help them if they learned to apply these methods and systems automatically. For example, when a girl hesitated over how many fours were in 24, the Y6 teacher reminded her of a previous tip: '*the best way to have worked that out would have been to go up your 4 times table (using fingers) – 4, 8, 12, – count in fours see how many fingers are up by the time you get to 24*'.

Another example was when children were asked to find the factors of a number. The Y6 teacher prompted them to '*work methodically – remember to use that system of asking yourself questions: Will one go into it? Will two go into it? Will three go into it? and so on*'.

Y6 teachers frequently informed children that learning tables by rote was a useful thing to do because when it came to number operations '*you simply know the answer and you can rely on it being accurate without having to calculate it over and over again*'.

SCIENCE

A Y6 teacher told children that a good learning strategy was to make connections with other facts already known and to compare known facts with new facts, thus learning how things were the same or different. The example she gave was of human reproduction and plant reproduction: '*basically male fertilizing female in humans and in flowers*'.

The strategy 'relaying ways of learning' was used throughout lessons. Lessons were peppered with advice about how to go about learning. Some teachers were in the habit of flagging up important information directly before they gave it by saying '*this is the bit of the lesson you must really listen to well*' or '*now you must really think about this next bit*' or '*it is important to concentrate, particularly when I pull the lesson together at the end*'.

In lessons where children were practising or consolidating something already taught, teachers (not surprisingly) referred more to the use of memory jogs than they did when teaching new content. In both types of lesson, teachers constantly stressed the important connection between listening and learning. Invariably, these messages about learning were transmitted to the whole class, although teachers were sometimes seen to repeat them to individuals when the children were working on activities.

This strategy was widely employed by both Y2 and Y6 teachers although few reported that they consciously used it. When observed, Y2 teachers stressed the importance of listening more than any other learning behaviour.

e) Modelling

Modelling involved the teachers in personally portraying what they wanted children to do. Teachers of both age groups described their belief in the importance of the teacher as model, the teacher behaving in a way that they desired the children to imitate: *'Teaching by example – seeing by example – me writing stories'*.

Besides being applied to teacher as writer, teachers also acted as exemplar of how to talk. As one expressed it:

'When a child gives a response like 'I <u>runned</u> down the shop' . . . I would say 'Oh, so you <u>ran</u> down to the shop?' – putting their language back to them in a role modelling correct tense'.

f) Demonstrating

Demonstrating was a practical way of illustrating something in order to make it really clear to children. Demonstrating was usually used to show children how to tackle a task, how to use an item of equipment (or how not to use it), how to make a construction of some kind or how to record something.

Demonstrating in different lesson contexts

ENGLISH – HANDWRITING

Teachers used demonstration when teaching handwriting. Generally they believed in actively doing it in front of children; *'going through it with them – the right way of where to start and where to finish'*. A Y6 teacher reported:

> *That's something you can class-teach, on the blackboard, a row of this letter, a row of that letter and show them how to join up certain letters.*

Although both Y2 and Y6 teachers were observed demonstrating to the whole class, Y2 were more likely to work one-to-one with a child on the formation of letters, sometimes holding a child's hand as they manipulated the pencil or providing a correctly formed letter for the child to write over or copy.

ENGLISH – WRITING

In Y2 classes 'shared writing' was a way of combining children's contributions with the teacher's own contributions to develop a model story or poem while commanding the attention of a whole group or class. Y6 teachers described how they demonstrated on the blackboard the use of speech marks, the layout of dialogue and the subdivision of text into paragraphs.

ENGLISH – READING

Teachers acted as model readers on some occasions. For example, while working with a child with learning difficulties, a Y6 teacher showed him how she was using pictures and other cues to decode words; a Y2 teacher followed the words she was reading aloud with her finger and looked up as a sign she had finished reading the words on each page, while another demonstrated how to find a word in the dictionary by doing it herself.

MATHS

In maths, teachers demonstrated methods – showing how to carry out a number operation either to the whole class on the board or to ability groups gathered round a flip chart or to individuals directly into their books. Often teachers gave a running commentary as they demonstrated how to calculate the first few examples on a worksheet, before children went on to complete it. Teachers demonstrated how to lay out sums, how to use a ruler, scales and other apparatus, how to construct a 3D shape, how to draw graphs accurately with correct labelling – usually to the whole class in the first instance and often repeated when the children had begun on the tasks, if individuals needed further support.

With children who were finding it difficult to get going on open-ended maths investigations, teachers modelled systems telling children '*I'll show you a way I know*' but encouraging children to explore other ways. In one Y2 classroom at the end of a lesson, the teacher demonstrated an unsystematic way of going about finding patterns thus informing children what NOT to do in subsequent lessons. The same teacher, in response to a child's incorrect suggestion that the subdivisions on a scale represented half a centimetre (when they really represented a tenth – a millimetre) carried out his suggestion – counted up the scale in halves to demonstrate that he was, in fact, wrong.

In a Y6 classroom, during a lesson on probability involving 10 different coloured marbles, the teacher constantly rephrased children's responses modelling the correct mathematical language. For example when a child said (correctly) that there was a five out of ten chance of getting a red marble, the teacher agreed saying *'Yes an even chance'*.

SCIENCE

Y6 teachers explained the importance of modelling the use of correct scientific vocabulary and terminology when talking to groups of children, especially while they were engaged in experimenting and testing. In many instances teachers were observed to model the correct use of science apparatus.

Demonstrating was used at the beginning of a lesson when the teacher was commanding the attention of the whole class and had arranged seating so that all children could see; also in the middle part of a lesson when the teacher was interacting with individual children and sometimes at the end of a lesson as a kind of reminder or 'last opportunity' to see how something should have been done (e.g. when teachers reworked sums children had already completed).

Teachers reported using demonstration more when a lesson involved new knowledge or understanding and less when children were consolidating something they had learned through practise. When children were trying to apply something they had learned, too much teacher demonstration was seen by teachers as antithetical to learning.

Modelling and demonstrating were described and used equally by teachers of both age groups. Both Y2 and Y6 teachers gave personal one-to-one demonstrations to children while they were circulating, although Y2 teachers did this more often, possibly because Y2 children were at an earlier stage of learning skills. Y6 teachers were more likely to give a blackboard demonstration to the whole class.

g) Conveying examples of children's work

Teachers found ways of conveying examples of children's methods or children's work to the rest of the class. A teacher might ask a child to show a method they had been using because it was a good method. In the words of a Y6 teacher:

> *You are using a child as a model for the rest of the children . . . the child's ways of working, how they can effectively use their skill, or have understood a concept.*

Alternatively, the teacher might ask the child to read out something good they had written or she herself might read out or show and describe a piece or extract of work, conveying it as an example of good work.

> *I would make a point of holding up the [good] examples and saying . . . this was really good because. . . .*
>
> (Y6 teacher)

The intention was to help other children better understand what was expected of them and one or two teachers explained that they ask the children to describe their methods because children often speak in a language which is very accessible to their peers.

A teacher might use this strategy to consolidate teaching, to show an example of work that contained everything the teacher had asked for, while another reason for using this strategy was to motivate or maintain interest, usually part way through an investigation – by showing work already done children were given fresh ideas and spurred on. A fourth and less direct function was to give kudos to individuals whose self esteem the teacher particularly wanted to raise:

> *Like Ben today for his idea . . . getting him to come out and write it up . . . that's praise and that's like saying – yes, you are part of the club . . . your decision is valid.*

One or two teachers also described conveying examples of a common problem using children's work. As one expressed it: 'Taking one person's problem and talking about it with other people to whom it may also be useful'.

In general we noticed that teachers did not as a rule identify the person with the problem, but rather noticed the problem and used it to teach something afresh or give a demonstration of some kind. On the odd observed occasion where teachers conveyed examples of a common problem using examples of children's mistakes, the teachers were invariably sensitive, often asking the child's permission to use the example. One such example follows.

The teacher was giving the whole Y6 class some feedback on the stories they had written. She asked Chan to read out his work, a really excellent 'fable'. Everyone clapped. The teacher beckoned to Chan to come and sit by her and, with an arm round him she said to the class 'What I love about Chan is that I don't have to put a lot of red circles round his work . . . except . . . (smiling and in a warm tone) . . . he sometimes leaves 'ed' off the ends of his verbs. The children nodded to each other, recognising this for themselves. Chan nodded with resignation. The teacher re-read Chan's story aloud, stressing the wonderful 'vibrant' verbs he had used while at the same time showing him where 'ed' should have come. At the end of the story, a voice from the class remarked, 'the moral of the fable is not clear'. The teacher agreed and showed Chan that she had made the same written comment on his work – 'Chan you really need to state that clearly. You just simply say 'And the moral of this story is . . .'. She asked everyone to clap again in appreciation of Chan's story.

Conveying examples of work in different types of lesson

Teachers used this strategy in all subjects. In maths, several teachers (of both age groups) reported asking children to explain their own successful computation methods to the rest of the class with a view to helping others to learn. For example, a Y6 teacher asked a boy to explain how he worked out the correct answer to a subtraction sum. (The teacher later explained: 'I use the way he understands and communicates a method as a model for the rest of the children'.) A few teachers repeatedly turned to the same (able) child to carry out this kind of demonstration for the benefit of others.

In English, observed instances of teaching through conveying examples were: asking a good reader to read aloud while the other children followed the text; writing up plausible and useful suggestions for 'good opening sentences' taken from group brainstorming; asking children to read out their poems (which had fulfilled the teacher's instructions to use lots of adjectives); showing a boy's well-formed handwriting sample.

In relation to teaching science a Y6 teacher explained:

In science, children can demonstrate an experiment and show other children how they did it and that will trigger other children to think . . . Oh, I could have tried it that way.

In our observations of lessons we witnessed teachers conveying examples of 'good' thinking in science. For example, at the end of an investigation into mirrors and light, the teacher asked a boy *'What did we find out then, Carl?'* to which the boy was able to explain to the class the fact that the fewer images appeared, the greater the angle. In another instance, when children had been investigating the use of materials in a design-and-make session, the teacher asked a pair to show how their *'machine to separate lentils'* worked and she described why the model was successful.

One function of this strategy appeared to be to motivate or maintain interest. We observed an instance of this when a Y2 teacher commended a boy's methods of finding a pattern, saying *'Right, someone has found something very exciting and very simple. Listen to him, if you're interested'.* The boy presented his theory clearly to the class. On another occasion, in a Y6 classroom, once the children had started writing a story, the teacher walked round, reading out some of their titles and showing enthusiasm: *'Batman Surprise – that sounds interesting – I'm coming to read that'; 'The wind behind the door . . . spooky! . . . worth a read!'*

In a third example the teacher had collected together 'good story starts' gleaned from the work of the class and had used these to help children to analyse all the different ways of starting a story. She motivated the children by reporting *'all these extracts have been written by authors in this room!'.*

Teachers used this strategy at all stages in lessons. However, there was more opportunity for sharing work in lessons where children were engaged upon the same task and in lessons which had a clear plenary. There was less use of this strategy in lessons where children worked on individual workcards at different levels, where the teacher worked with individuals (as in one-to-one reading sessions) or where the teacher focused her attention on teaching a group in the middle part of lessons.

At the end of lessons, teachers might convey examples of good working habits. For example, a Y6 teacher described how he would *'highlight something that a particular child had done that had moved the group forward'* or *'highlight how a child had managed to pull the group back on task'.*

After marking, teachers might save particularly good pieces of written work and bring them into the introduction of a later lesson. As a Y2 teacher explained: *'I will use what I consider to be good pieces of work as targets so that the children have some idea of what the expectations are – to work towards'.*

In lessons where children were consolidating something already taught or practising skills, teachers frequently used this strategy as a teaching technique, asking members of the class to demonstrate good methods and viable solutions to the whole class or picking out particular examples for the benefit of all.

The strategy of 'conveying examples of children's methods and work' was usually preceded by assessment of some kind (for example, observation, making a mental assessment note or analysing work) and it was usually followed by descriptive feedback about why examples had been chosen, why they were good and how they matched what the teacher had been looking for. At times the examples were used to stimulate children's own examination of why they were good.

Teachers of both age groups used this strategy in the same ways; there was no difference between Y6 and Y2 here. Teachers who organised a plenary session in lessons were more likely to use this part of the time to convey and describe examples of children's work than teachers who did not draw children together at the end of a lesson.

II   Reinforcing

We identified five strategies that teachers were using to reinforce learning and, not surprisingly, these strategies often involved repeating something. Teachers recapped and revised bits of knowledge and, to give emphasis to important points while they were talking, repeated their own words. They also repeated practical demonstrations.

We categorised these reinforcement strategies as:

- Reminding;
- Repeating;
- Re-demonstrating;
- Directing to further practising; and
- Directing a child to help or teach another child.

a) Reminding

This reinforcement strategy was observed to be one of the most predominant verbal strategies used throughout lessons. Teachers felt it necessary to give constant reminders of the key bits of information or the key skills that they had decided children should possess.

At the beginning of lessons, teachers of both age groups stood at the front and through recapping, reciting or summarising, reminded children of bits of knowledge and information previously taught. Many of our teachers (both age groups) added visual reminders by writing up words and diagrams as they were talking. More interactively, they used specific questions aimed at drawing out particular answers, which would act as a kind of recap. Although assessment may not have been the main intention here teachers were often able to gauge the general level of understanding of the group and this resulted in even more reminding.

In the middle of lessons, when teachers were circulating, they would often stop the class and remind them of the objective of the lesson. They reminded individuals about all kinds of things as they observed them at work. In this context, reminding was the outcome of an assessment. (*'Remember you are supposed to be keeping all your letters on the line'*.) Reminding doubled as feedback in this context in that teachers might also be specifying a way to improve.

Recapping, reciting and summarising were also used at the end of lessons when children were drawn together to be reminded of the key facts of the lesson.

When teachers were introducing children to a concept for the first time they gave frequent reminders, at intervals throughout their introductions, of the main facts that were being learned. In contrast, teachers spent only a short time on introductory reminders in lessons where children would be practising something already taught. When lessons involved practising something, teachers invited children to use memory jogging techniques they had taught them (for example, to use a catch phrase to remember how to 'borrow' a ten in subtraction) or to use a framework given as an aid (for example, a structure or system to follow for writing a story). Reminding was used in all subjects observed and equally by Y2 and Y6 teachers.

b) Repeating

When we looked closely at our observations and the transcripts of teachers' talk during lessons, it was clear that teachers used a lot of word repetition as a reinforcement strategy. Throughout the introduction to lessons, when they were commanding the attention of the whole class, they frequently repeated their own words (verbatim or slightly rephrased) to reinforce the lesson objectives and teaching points that they thought were particularly important. For example, one Y6 teacher repeated *'we are thinking today about what makes a good story*' seven times within the first minutes of her introduction and another repeated '*[this is] how a plant makes a seed*' three times within seconds, during an interactive lesson where children were observing flower heads.

In the middle of lessons, while teachers were moving around looking at children's work, they would often stop the class and repeat verbatim a list of instructions given at the beginning of the lesson (such as a list of steps to go through). At the end of lessons, again to the whole class, they often repeated key words and meanings as a way of confirming what should have been learned. The function of repeating words was to make things as clear as possible for the children.

Teachers also repeated themes in their delivery. For example, when a Y2 teacher was teaching children to interpret diagrams from her drawings on the whiteboard, she peppered her input with variations on the theme of clues:

> I'm going to give you a clue;
> I'm drawing a line – this might help you to answer;
> I'm going to put some clues on the diagram;
> I'll use the ruler and that will help you to see;
> What clue would I need to put on, if it's centimetres?

Teachers appeared to use repetition to the same degree in lessons which contained new knowledge and in lessons where children were practising something already taught. There was no difference in the way Y2 and Y6 teachers used this strategy.

c) Re-demonstrating

Re-demonstrating was used to show children (again) how to tackle a task, how to use an item of equipment, how to make a construction of some kind or how to record something. Teachers of both age groups described and were seen to use this strategy in the same ways.

Re-demonstrating was a strategy used both in lessons where children were learning something new and when they were practising something taught previously. Re-demonstrating was used in maths and English lessons for both age groups but to a much lesser degree in Y6 science (possibly because teachers allowed more exploration).

The usual context for this strategy was when teachers (circulating) repeated to individuals or small groups something they had shown to the whole class earlier and after they had made some kind of judgment about the ways in which the children were working. In the words of a Y6 teacher:

> *You come up to an individual and they have not managed to extrapolate from the class bit of teaching exactly what you are talking about – then you go through all that range of techniques with them.*

Often with children who were slower to learn, teachers would repeat the demonstration but present it in a different way, for example, by bringing in some supportive apparatus. This kind of intervention was sometimes teacher-orchestrated and sometimes in response to a child seeking help.

Re-demonstrating nearly always followed assessment. Re-demonstration frequently came after teachers had taken work home to be marked and had noticed that the majority of children were misunderstanding something crucial.

At times re-demonstration was accompanied by verbal feedback which negotiated a route to improve something. For example, a Y2 teacher invited a child to compare her own formation of letters with the model provided on the whiteboard and asked her to notice the difference and correct her work.

At other times written feedback followed assessment and preceded re-demonstration. For example, when teachers (both age groups) wrote 'come and talk to me' in children's exercise books. This often meant that the teacher would show again some number operation or spelling pattern which the child needed to learn.

d) Directing to further practising

Teachers decided that all or some children needed to acquire further knowledge, skills or understandings and so directed them to further work or further practice. Children might be directed to practise more examples of something they had not grasped, directed to a more challenging activity or simply directed to follow up something outside of school ('*Tonight for homework I want you to see what mathematical shapes you can find around the house*'). By its nature, this strategy was invariably used in lessons when children were consolidating something previously taught.

After marking maths work at home teachers were seen, at the beginning of a new lesson, to redirect individuals (who were getting a lot wrong) towards easier work. If the majority of children had turned in disappointing work, the teacher often provided a whole-class lesson on the same topic, followed by everybody practising – and this linked directly with the strategies of reminding and re-demonstrating.

In the middle of maths lessons, when teachers were moving around, it was common for them to jot down for struggling children further sums of the kind giving trouble. To individuals whom the teacher knew to be able, they might give further, more challenging assignments.

Sometimes teachers held a general philosophy of 'practise, practise and more practise' and this would lead them to constantly get the whole class using and applying a particular skill (particularly in relation to number operations, spelling and reading).

Frequently, when children had finished the task expected of them in any subject, teachers would direct them to practise some necessary skill as a way of filling their time. Practising handwriting was common but often children were sent to carry out research in the classroom or school library – to read books from a display of non-fiction or to find information using CD ROM. On the occasions when children asked teachers general knowledge questions, they were often directed to go and find the answer for themselves. Practising went on after school in the form of homework, mostly but not exclusively, for Y6.

e) Directing a child to help or teach another child

Teachers generally believed that, quite a lot of the time, children would be helping and passing on knowledge and methods to each other without the suggestion of the teacher; this was especially likely when children sat together in groups. However, all the teachers described the strategy of directing children to help/teach each other but explained that they would use it only occasionally. Sometimes children were placed in the teacher role and sometimes in the learner role. Children placed in the teacher role had some ability or some know-how about learning. Children placed in the learner role needed support, information or learning tips. Teachers explained that they tried their best to vary the roles so that children had experience of both, depending on individual expertise and so that children's self esteem was preserved.

Teachers believed that children, being learners themselves, were able to articulate and break down what they had learned into steps that would benefit other children. Teachers mostly organised children in pairs for this 'teaching' activity but there were also occasions when a child addressed a larger group or even the whole class. One Y6 teacher moved particular individuals to sit in certain groups because they had a special skill in helping other children and were competent in writing skills themselves. This was a classroom 'norm' and the children accepted it.

When a child addressed the whole class or a group, the function was for a child to teach something they knew. In one instance the teacher had asked an able artist to take charge of a group working with particular materials; in the other instance, the teacher explained:

> I have had a child stand up and do a 40-minute lesson on percentages . . . what he did manage to do was to teach a mixed ability class about percentages because he had a different way of doing it than I did and it was successful.

In the paired context, one function of this strategy was repetition of teaching by a peer, as explained by a Y6 teacher: 'What did I do today? The moment I had some children who understood how to do the task, and some who didn't – I immediately put them together'.

Another function was the provision of descriptive feedback by a peer, described by another Y6 teacher as:

> One child will read through another child's piece of work and suggest ways in which the child can move it on.

Another reason teachers used this strategy was that they believed it promoted thinking and reinforced learning in the child/teacher. As a Y2 teacher expressed it:

> It means they've got to think about what they've learnt in order to tell someone else about it.

Lessons in which children were asked to teach others

Teachers explained that they made most use of this strategy in reading, IT, and writing but there were occasions when children were asked to explain scientific and mathematical ideas to others.

Several teachers of both age groups reported that they put children together in pairs for reading (although we observed this also happening in four cases of investigative science in Y6.) In this context one reader would usually be a slightly better reader than the other and the intention was that the less able child could learn from the other's strategies. One Y6 teacher had passed on teaching techniques to children who would play the teacher role and described it as:

We've tried to get them to do the same kind of questioning technique that I would do and . . . [say] 'look at that again'; 'look at the first two letters'; 'get your mouth ready to say it'; 'you've seen that word already on the page before, so have a think about what it would be'; [point and say] 'that word sounds like that one'; 'put your fingers over that and split up the word'.

Teachers reported asking a child who had learned a particular technical computing skill to pass on their knowledge to another child (such as teaching them how to save a document).

In writing, the practice of 'editing' was reported mostly by Y6 teachers. Children were directed to edit each other's work, *vis-à-vis* spelling, punctuation and general ideas. Children were encouraged to take their peers' comments seriously.

In both age groups able writers were asked to scribe for less skilled peers so that the latters' ideas were sure to be expressed on paper. As one teacher explained:

Children who can't write, it doesn't mean to say necessarily that they aren't good at ideas, but you may not get to see the ideas because of the [writing] process slowing them down.

There were three contexts for this strategy – the middle of lessons when children were working on activities, lessons when the whole lesson consisted of paired work, and lessons devoted to children working individually through a graded workcard system. In that context a Y6 teacher explained how the strategy helped her:

. . . in maths, if I am tied up trying to explain something to somebody, say in the maths scheme, and another child is stuck . . . and I know someone else has done that card, I will ask them to teach it . . .

When teachers used this strategy it was based on their assessment of what some children knew and understood that other children did not. In this way, it was a teaching strategy used after observing or questioning.

Teachers of both age groups explained that they occasionally used the strategy of directing children to help/teach each other. In our very few observations of the strategy in action, Y2 teachers were less likely to make this overt but as likely as Y6 to put children into pairs so that they could learn from each other. It is clear from the literature that getting children to help and teach each other is a strategy that can support children's learning's, since a child who is slightly more knowledgeable can help 'bridge the gap' for another child. The teachers aimed to find ways of doing just this, which brings us to the third group of teaching strategies – those used to support learning.

III   Supporting learning

We also identified strategies which go beyond the definition of teaching given at the start of the chapter that teachers were using to support learning. These included verbal strategies introduced into conversations with children at appropriate moments when there was a chance of extending children's learning, the practical inclusion of props or equipment at a salient moment and the modification of teachers' language and/or the content of their input to take account of individual learners.

We categorised these supportive strategies as:

- Bringing different strands of information together;
- Using questioning to promote thinking;
- Providing visual and audio props; and
- Giving different treatment.

a) Bringing different strands of information together

This strategy involved teachers in bringing together and linking something previously taught with something new; bringing together school learning with 'everyday experiences'; highlighting differences between things and bringing elements of different subject areas together. Teachers of both age groups reported that, when they were passing on new knowledge of some kind to children, they always tried to connect something taught in the past to this new knowledge. In the words of one Y2 teacher:

> With new content you are obviously recapping and revisiting other aspects before you are ready to move on. You remind them of what they were doing last week because it links onto the next thing anyway.

This technique gave an opportunity for revising what had been taught but was also intended to reassure children and make new learning seem less daunting. On occasion teachers even described how new learning was to fit into an overall plan:

I have got a definite plan of where we are going next and I will inform children where we are going to go so that they've got a picture in their mind of how things are linking up.

Teachers stressed the importance of bringing together school learning with everyday experiences – so that children could see links between learning and life. An example given by a Y2 teacher was practising writing letters by inviting children to write letters to real people asking for information. An example of this in action was when a Y6 teacher invited all her children to look at the labels on their clothing to see how percentages were used to show the composition of different materials.

By highlighting the differences between things, teachers brought together different elements of information. For example, they described the different characteristics of pieces of work that are 'art' and pieces of work that are 'scientific diagrams' or pieces of writing that are 'stories' and those that are 'poems', or books that are fiction and books that are non-fiction, or shapes that are 'circles' and shapes that are 'spheres'.

Teachers explained how they brought together strands of information from different subjects. For example, when working with children on handling data, they drew out the similarity between graphs produced in maths lessons, charts produced in science lessons and data bases used in IT lessons and explained how patterns could be detected by manipulating data in all these areas.

One Y6 teacher who was observed over a number of days used the same stimulus to link information from a number of learning experiences: her children made an observational drawing of a flower, wrote a poem about the same flower then dissected it. In her interactions with children during the latter two activities, the teacher constantly connected what they had learned from the three activities.

Bringing different strands of information together in different lessons

MATHS

Specifically in relation to maths, teachers brought different strands of information together when they:

> informed children about links and connections between addition and multiplication – indicating how adding a set of numbers and multiplying two numbers can give the same answer;

informed children about connections between number operations and work in measurement, shape and other areas of maths. For example, how five out of ten as a fraction (number) can be expressed as 'even chance' in probability (data handling);

invited children to discover connections between different aspects of mathematical learning by setting problems or investigations;

invited children to see things in more than one way (for example, expressing numbers and their factors as shapes on squared paper – seeing numbers as rectangles or squares);

combined the teaching of skills (for example, how to measure) with the development of concepts (for example, an understanding of 'longer and shorter').

ENGLISH

Specifically in relation to English, teachers brought different strands of information together when they:

helped children to make links between what they see and what they hear by drawing their attention to both sound patterns and visual patterns in words;

invited children to discover connections between writing and reading. For example, reminding children of stories they had read and connecting the task of writing to an analysis of those stories;

combined two aspects of teaching. For example, demonstrating handwriting 'joins' while simultaneously teaching a particular blend of sounds;

linked information about how to write a story with information about using a plan or framework.

SCIENCE

Y6 teachers believed that aspects of physics (forces, energy) seem to be difficult for children to understand and they reported bringing information about physical processes into as many other lessons as possible. ('*You have got to use every opportunity to refer to it, touch on it, even if you*

are not specifically doing a topic on it'.) In science, Y6 teachers brought
different strands of information together when they drew parallels. (For
example between previous sex education information on human reproduction with work in hand on pollination.)

The strategy of bringing different strands of information together
was used at different stages in lessons. At the beginning of lessons,
directed at the whole class, teachers often recapped previous knowledge before introducing new material. At the end of lessons, teachers
were observed to bring together all the strands of information given in
that lesson, to *'put all that knowledge and information into some sort of
order in their heads'*. Brief summaries of the whole lesson were given to
the whole class: *'we talk about what we have learned and what we haven't
learned, what we would like to enforce and where we are going next'*.

Teachers of both age groups described using this strategy quite consciously. A common aim among teachers was to help children to make
links between different things they were learning.

b) Using questioning to promote thinking

Questioning was a strategy used on many occasions by teachers. The
purposes of questioning differed. Sometimes questioning was used as
an assessment technique (see 'oral testing' and 'delving' in the next
chapter) and sometimes it was used in teaching.

Teachers would throw out open-ended questions to the class or groups
and would not expect answers to the questions; they asked the questions as an indirect mode of teaching to encourage them to think. In
the words of one teacher:

> *If there is something that they have to think about a lot, rather than me
> just tell them how to do it, I would pose a question in such a way that
> it leads them to think . . . 'What would you do?' 'What if you did it this
> way?' So I am starting to get them to think . . . starting thinking and
> reflecting for themselves.*

The function of this type of questioning was, then, to promote thinking and theorising or, as one Y2 teacher expressed it: giving a kind of
suggested structure through questioning, by asking, for example – *'What
do you think you'll need to help you. . . .'* *'How are you going to make that?'*;
'How could you change that in order to make it better?' The purpose of
using this strategy was explained by another Y2 teacher thus: *'By
questioning you hope they will think . . . if I did so-and-so that might work'*.
Although teachers did not necessarily expect answers, children would

of course give them. The answers were usually given positive evaluative feedback, and an instruction to try ('*Good. Try that idea*').

We observed this type of questioning to be used chiefly in contexts (all subjects, but mainly maths and science) in which children had been given an investigative task – exploratory with no fixed answers, for example, an investigation of the properties of shapes, a design-and-make activity using different materials or an analytical task – for example where children were asked to think about what makes a good story or indeed in sessions where children were expected to write freely.

Teachers would usually use this type of questioning as they toured the room when children were working, briefly observing children's efforts and putting in the odd question to set children thinking. For example in science: '*Why do you think that happens?*'; '*How could you test that theory?*'. In poetry writing: '*Any ideas for words to describe the texture of the leaf?*'

We observed a number of instances of this questioning, mainly in science in Y6. For example:

> During an investigation into friction, the teacher, observing one group, picked up different bits of apparatus and asked, '*Can you think how you might use this in your construction?*'
>
> During a mirror investigation, the teacher pointed to what they had already written, then asked a pair, '*So for 45 degrees you can see eight images. With 90 degrees, are you expecting to see eight? What do you think is happening?*'
>
> When children were designing a machine to separate lentils from split peas, the children examined a group's model and queried, '*This is interesting – how do you stop it spilling?*'
>
> When children were testing heart rates, the teacher asked a group to theorise, '*Why might we do that test again – why might scientists do things twice?*'
>
> Teachers did not ask the same question of all pairs or groups but rather, based on gauging the level of a group's general understanding, they adapted their questions.

There were occasions when teachers used this type of questioning when commanding the attention of the whole class. For example, a Y2 teacher described asking questions at the end of a design-and-make session: '*Why did this one work? Why did this one not work?*'. Her purpose here was to get children to analyse the strengths and weaknesses of different designs.

When teachers used this strategy while touring the room it was based on their assessment of how children were proceeding with a task. In this way, it was a teaching strategy used after checking, observing, eavesdropping and gauging the (national curriculum) level. When teachers used the strategy at the end of lessons it was often used in conjunction with the other strategy – 'conveying examples of work' and in a way this type of questioning was a means by which the teacher negotiated with children why work was good.

A number of teachers (mainly Y2) used a lesson pattern which involved them in focusing their teaching on one group during the activities (see Chapter 2). These teachers were as likely to ask questions to promote thinking but less likely to walk away leaving the children to think. Rather they took the children's answers or suggestions and built them into their teaching, moving the whole group on in their understanding.

Teachers of both age groups used questioning to promote thinking. Not surprisingly this type of questioning was not used in lessons where children were practising a routine skill (e.g. handwriting).

c) Providing visual and audio props

'*I can't really do anything without visual clues*' reported one of our teachers and this seemed to resonate with several teachers as we watched them at work.

Many of the teachers used drama, mime and change of voice to illustrate the points they were making and this made learning 'more fun'. In a lesson on 'probability' a Y6 teacher performed a conjuring trick – three cups and a pea under one of them – to prompt children to guess the chances of finding the pea. Two teachers had a habit of doodling on the whiteboard as part of introductions and plenaries, illustrating the various contributions children made. For example when one Y6 boy suggested that a good way to structure a poem was to '*use your five senses*', the teacher drew eyes, nose, ears, mouth and fingers as the boy listed sight, smell, sound, taste and touch. This reinforced the points in a visual way and also amused the class. A Y6 teacher made up a little character with her fingers as 'Bertie the Bee' and in his voice illustrated how insects are attracted to pollen. 'Landing' on a real tulip head, she named each part of the flower as carpel, stamen, anthers, nectary. Real things were, in fact, a feature of most of our classrooms – objects were often on hand for the use of children and teachers.

At times, in an attempt to add to a child's learning, teachers sought out pictures in books to illustrate what they were talking about and brought them into their interactions with children at the precise moment they were needed. In a few Y6 classrooms, teachers used children's work already on display for the same purpose. Videos were used both as stimulus to a new topic and at instances over a term to help children consolidate learning.

As mentioned earlier, teachers of both age groups provided formats and structures for children to follow, particularly in writing and these acted as a skeleton for a story or factual writing. In science also, Y6 teachers provided grids and table formats to facilitate children's recording of their observations.

Two teachers had a particular habit of using children to represent things – for example bringing children to the front of the class to represent the planets or lining children up to give some idea of the length of something. Many teachers asked children to convey examples of how they carried out number work by writing on the board. One Y2 teacher always asked children to 'draw letter sounds in the air' as part of practising phonics.

It appeared that many teachers had planned the use of visual props before a lesson to stimulate interest but, equally, teachers introduced these at pertinent moments with individuals as they were needed and in an attempt to take learning forward.

As with visual props, all our teachers planned in advance the maths and science equipment children would need to carry out a task or experiment. It was a strong characteristic of these classrooms that children had hands-on experience.

d) Giving different treatment

Because the teachers believed that children learn in different ways, they treated them differently. They were concerned to use language accessible to individuals and to give feedback that was suited to them. When touring the room and working with different children, the teaching content might be the same but the interaction would be different according to what the teacher knew about each child.

Sometimes teachers would ask questions directly to individuals in a whole class group – they reported that they carefully tailored their questions to get the best from each child. They also considered how they would give feedback – the tone they would use, how much they would criticise or praise.

In practical terms, one Y6 teacher set up a support network for a boy who had reached his class without being able to read – extra time was given after school, with his parents and one-to-one, going beyond what was offered to those children who could read. Similarly, it was a feature of most classrooms that Primary helpers, well-briefed, would work with children who found learning difficult, giving them more concentrated attention than perhaps others in the class. In all classrooms, more able children were constantly pushed to more challenging tasks.

WHAT CAN WE LEARN FROM THE TEACHERS' CHOICE OF STRATEGIES?

To summarise, the teaching strategies used were:

I Informing

- Relaying knowledge;
- Explaining;
- Instructing;
- Relaying ways of learning;
- Modelling;
- Demonstrating; and
- Conveying examples of children's work.

II Reinforcing

- Reminding;
- Repeating;
- Re-demonstrating;
- Directing to further practising; and
- Directing a child to help or teach another child.

III Supporting learning

- Bringing different strands of information together;
- Using questioning to promote thinking;
- Providing visual and audio props; and
- Giving different treatment.

Our expert teachers believed they had an *active* role in the process of teaching and this coincided with what we observed: they worked intensively with full concentration whether it was with the whole class, groups or individual children; they rarely disengaged themselves. Expert teaching, then, entails the dynamic use of a range of strategies including verbal as well as practical demonstrative techniques.

Especially when topics are new to children, there is a clear role for the transmission of knowledge, provided this does not dominate the teacher's delivery for too long, and is backed by extended explanation and some modelling and demonstration. Facts and information should not be way beyond a child's experience and 'lectures' are not an effective mode of delivery, although step-by-step instructing in the basic skills of number, handwriting and grammar is necessary.

Describing strategies for learning (helping children to see ways of learning) is one characteristic of the expert teacher, as is taking time to model good learning habits and using the tactics of other learners as a teaching tool. The good teacher ensures that children consolidate what they learn in all subjects by reminding and repeating and emphasising learning points. There are times when directing children to extra practise is essential and careful use of child-to-child teaching can aid understanding in a number of activities.

Expert teaching implies a willingness to seek every possible way to clarify things for children and to extend their learning, bridging the gap between what they understand alone and what they might understand with the help of another. Crucially important is making connections and showing, for example, relationships between different areas of maths and between sounds and visual patterns of words, and drawing parallels among human, animal and plant processes in science. Carefully worded open questions (which do not sound like test questions) can promote thinking about (for example) why methods of working may have been unsuccessful (maths) or why some tests were not 'fair' (science). The good teacher will also get to know her children well, react to them in different ways according to their learning approaches and make wise decisions about the use of props and equipment that will help them to learn.

Lastly, the teaching strategies need to be set within a classroom ethos of support, sensitivity, acknowledgment and respect for what children themselves know and can contribute, as the chapter on learning will emphasise. We now turn to the assessment strategies we observed and teachers talked about.

Chapter 4

Assessment

INTRODUCTION

Teachers tend to carry out two types of assessment – formal and informal. Formal assessment, using standardised tests, SATs, baseline testing etc. is usually required by school policy, the LEA or government. Informal assessment, however, tends to be for teachers' own use, done when and how they choose, in order to check on children's learning and progress. This is what was described in the first chapter as formative assessment. In our observations and interviews with teachers we concentrated on informal assessment.

Assessment strategies used in the classroom

Throughout the early interviews teachers referred to informal assessment that goes on all the time in their minds during teaching and is rarely if ever recorded at the time; teachers are constantly making judgments about children, their learning strategies and their knowledge and understanding. All teachers described this kind of assessment. '*It's the stuff I'm doing all the time – I can't separate it,*' explained one. '*It's the much more personal assessment, knowing them as individuals, able to recognise from their faces whether they understand*', said another. '*Some of it's in my head, just going round in my head,*' reported a third.

As our visits progressed, however, teachers began to describe more specifically the assessment strategies they use in the classroom.

From these discussions with teachers and our observations of their teaching, we developed a definition of 'assessment' as

> the use of a verbal or non-verbal technique with or without the child present in order to make a judgment about the child, the child's strategies, skills or attainment.

Working with this definition, we were able to isolate teachers' strategies that were distinctly '*assessment strategies*' as opposed to '*teaching*' or '*giving feedback*'.

The assessment strategies that teachers described in their interviews were:

- using other teachers' records;
- using written tests;
- observing;
- questioning;
- getting a child to demonstrate;
- checking;
- listening;
- eavesdropping;
- marking;
- making a mental assessment note;
- gauging the level.

Our observations corroborated these strategies, but from the observations we were also able to specify other assessment strategies. Although teachers did not distinguish between different types of questioning, we identified different types and functions of teachers' questioning, enabling us to describe two further assessment strategies:

- questioning – 'oral testing' and
- questioning – 'delving'.

Similarly, although teachers did not break down 'gauging the level', we were able to distinguish three strategies:

- 'gauging the level' – assessing general level of understanding;
- 'gauging the level' – judging individual progress; and
- 'gauging the level' – looking at a range of work to make a judgement about National Assessment levels.

We also identified another strategy which we named:

- working out why a child has or has not achieved.

In the following sections, each of these strategies will be described, together with their function and use in different subjects and contexts.

a) Using other teachers' records

When asked if they used any particular assessment techniques at the beginning of the year, over half the teachers explained that they read children's records passed on from other teachers. They described this as an assessment technique, because they used it to make a judgment about the child's skills or attainment.

For three teachers the function of reading the records was to use the assessments to group the children. These teachers accepted the assessments of their colleagues. For the others who read records, the function is unclear as they preferred (along with the other teachers in the sample) to make their own assessments of children new to their class and this was done through testing anew, the 'fresh start' philosophy.

b) Using written tests

Most of the teachers used written tests – whether standardised tests, 'old SAT papers' or their own teacher-designed tests, including asking children to do a piece of unaided work.

Most teachers did some form of testing at the beginning of a new year and the results were used to make initial judgements of the ability of incoming children and to set up ability groups. Taking a sample of unaided writing was to diagnose common errors and then plan future teaching. As one Y6 teacher explained:

> 'With the writing sample, I do do quite an in-depth study of these . . . then work through various areas, ideas and skills'.

A quarter gave weekly tests of one sort or another to the whole class in mental maths and spelling, constantly testing basic skills, and in 15 schools teachers gave assessment tasks after a topic had been taught. When teachers gave these periodic tests, their function was to assess how well children were learning what was being taught. In this case, testing as an assessment strategy was used to inform a teacher's future teaching. When assessment tasks were given after a taught unit (for example, termly) teachers would make judgements about how much had been learned and whether to re-teach the topic. So, giving written tests was part of both formative and summative assessment.

Thirteen teachers explained that they set their own tests for the whole class in English, maths and (less often) science to decide whether children could apply what they had learned after a taught unit of study.

For this some Y6 teachers used extracts from past SAT papers. A Y2 teacher explained that she used test sheets from a commercial mathematics scheme to give to children after they had practised certain number operations. Sometimes a test took the form of teachers asking children to make or do something. For example, a Y6 teacher said she would assess how children used and applied maths by asking them to play a game and a Y2 teacher explained a science assessment task she might give:

> At the end of a unit of work, after six weeks of electricity, I tend to do an assessment which confirms what I already know but I try to link it into a challenge. I may say 'I want you to make me a 3D picture that will light up from the back'.

Although teachers spoke a lot about using written tests, we saw very little in over 100 lesson observations. We saw no use of standardised tests but we did observe other testing in maths and English. In maths, there were three instances of Y6 teachers giving 15-minute tests on the four rules of number at the end of lessons and three classrooms in which Y6 children systematically did tests after they had completed a set of scheme workcards. In one Y2 class, the teacher asked children who had been using a database to create their own list of questions to test whether they understood what the database could do. In all of these cases, feedback was given immediately afterwards: the mental arithmetic answers were read out by the teacher and children gave themselves ticks or crosses. Teachers explained what children had and hadn't achieved on the Y6 'scheme' maths tests and in the Y2 classroom.

In English, we observed two instances of story writing under test conditions, one in Y2 and one in Y6. Here, feedback was not given until the teacher had taken the work away, scrutinised it and marked it.

Overall Y6 teachers were more likely to use standardised tests than Y2 teachers and in general to do more testing.

c) Observing

Teachers implied that 'observing' had three senses – 'noticing', and the more focused 'following' and 'watching'.

In the first sense, observing as 'noticing' was about what teachers became aware of in the course of being with children learning; our data indicates that this type of observing was used by all our teachers. The things teachers noticed would often lead to focused observing i.e. observing in the second sense, of '*following*' a child's learning strategies more closely in order to diagnose what it was that was either helping or hindering the child's learning or what the child was able to do or understand. Observing in its third sense ('*watching*') was regularly used by teachers who found it helpful to build in time to round back and observe groups of children in order to make judgements about them against criteria for National Curriculum records.

Noticing took place in all subjects. While moving around and observing '*on the hoof*', teachers said they noticed whether children were on task; whether they were coping; who was interested in the work; who was copying; who was dominating group work; how children began to tackle a task; who seemed unable to get started; who was wasting time; who showed an understanding or knowledge; whose work could be used as an exemplar to the whole class.

Observing became a kind of non-verbal '*monitoring*' of children's application, pace and learning strategies. At times, however, the teacher might give a teaching point to the whole class if she wanted them all to be aware of something she may have seen in passing.

There were certain times when teachers found it necessary to concentrate on a child's learning strategies and *follow* what was happening. Teachers described how they used focused observing when they had some cause for concern about behaviour or learning, or when they felt there was a need for more evidence of children's performance, particularly in speaking and listening, using and applying maths, experimenting and investigating in science. Examples included following the antics of one child whose behaviour was becoming unacceptable; looking at the working relationships and roles in particular pairs; observing how a child was holding a pen for handwriting; studying a child's learning behaviour. In the last case, one of the Y2 teachers explained that focused observing was essential '*so that you know when a child is at that point, ready to discover something*'; the teacher could then move in with questioning to promote thinking or relay new knowledge. In this case assessment by observation was followed by teaching.

Observation to assess children against National Assessment criteria was observation in the sense of *watching* often to assess Attainment Target 1 in the core subjects. For example, one Y6 teacher made a point of assessing Speaking and Listening every time children were handling historical artifacts and, in similar vein, a Y2 teacher assessed Speaking and Listening (as well as musical skills and group dynamics) while children were composing music in groups. The teachers also reported that observations were particularly useful to assess how children were using and applying number skills to practical problems (two other Y2 teachers frequently deployed classroom assistants to make observation notes about children when they were 'using and applying' a skill for the first time so that any misunderstandings could be picked up as soon as possible). These teachers explained that to allow them to carry out the observations they had to encourage a degree of independence in the learners. In contrast, 11 teachers explained that they could not plan to stand back and observe children because (in both age groups) they found themselves in great demand from the children.

Hearing children read was the context in which we most often witnessed teachers using observation as an assessment technique. They observed how individuals tackled print (for example, whether they were reading from left to right, using fingers to point to words, hiding parts of word to help them read). This careful observation, or *following*, was more prevalent when teachers withdrew children from busy classrooms or organised quiet activities for other children. (When teachers allowed interruptions from other children they were less likely to carefully observe children's tactics, rather they just listened to them read). In the majority of cases, teachers gave instant feedback and specified how a child might improve – for example a teacher observed that a child was relying too much on one reading strategy, pointed this out and explained other strategies, modelling how they could be used. Here assessment by observation was followed by feedback and teaching. During or after these reading sessions, teachers usually made assessment notes about individual progress.

Some teachers had a pattern of touring the room to *watch* when the children were set to activities. In the case of practical tasks in maths or science, teachers often paused at groups and observed how individuals were using equipment or apparatus or how they were solving construction problems. Sometimes teachers intervened and suggested a better way of doing something but sometimes they left children alone to experiment and discover better ways for themselves. In the case of handwriting, some teachers observed how children were forming letters. This was followed by teaching which implied specifying a better way – the teacher might model correct formation of letters for children then direct them to extra practise.

When teachers spent longer watching a group it was usually science or maths investigative group work and teachers reported that they had been assessing children's collaboration, their investigative skills and their manipulation of materials.

We noticed no differences between Y2 and Y6 teachers in their use of observation. There were differences however, among individuals, with some doing much more diagnosis through observation than others and some giving themselves more opportunity for closer observation through their classroom organisation and management.

d) Questioning

All 24 teachers reported using questioning as an assessment strategy, either with individuals or with groups. With a group, and often at the beginning of a new topic, questioning was used to gauge the level of 'what children already know' so that the teacher could judge how to pitch the teaching; this was not assessing what individuals knew. At the end of a lesson teachers reported using questioning to check what the group had learned. With individuals, teachers reported touring the room, working with individuals and using questioning to 'see what they have grasped', elicit personal understanding, diagnose misunderstandings and 'ascertain the approach they are taking to the task'.

As explained earlier we identified two types of questioning teachers used for assessment purposes: 'oral testing' and 'delving'.

• Oral testing

A common strategy observed in both Y2 and Y6 classrooms was 'oral testing'. By this we mean asking questions that require a correct answer, either quiz-like closed questions requiring a short answer ('How many grammes in a kilogramme?'; 'What letter comes after "V"?') or questions, still closed but designed to elicit a longer and more explanatory, yet correct, answer ('Why is there so much pollen on those stamens?').

The function of oral testing at whole-class level was to judge what children had retained from previous lessons. At the beginning of lessons, it acted also as a kind of quick revision for children in preparation for the imminent task. Within the whole-class setting, another function of oral testing was to judge what specific individuals had learned and remembered. As one teacher explained it: 'I direct questions at certain children to give me a feel for what they, in particular, have been able to take in'.

When working with individuals, oral testing might serve the function of a 'formal' assessment of what a child knew and understood in relation to NC programmes of study, and teachers might prepare a list of written questions to ask individuals as they toured the room during the middle of lessons. An indirect use of oral testing was when teachers used it in a 'corrective' way, spot-questioning individuals who did not seem to be listening. In the words of one teacher: *I might include some direct question to those who don't appear to be actively participating*.

Oral testing was used in all subjects. We observed teachers using the strategy in lessons on maths, phonics, science, in lessons devoted to punctuation and in lessons in which teachers read stories or extracts to children. It was used at all stages in a lesson, beginning, middle or end and it was used in different types of lesson.

In lesson introductions oral testing for quick revision was widely observed. Teachers questioned children about facts as well as about ways of doing things. In Y6, teachers asked what children already knew, parts of speech, parts of the body, parts of a flower, days in a week and weeks in a year; about working out percentages, working out subtraction sums; and about fair testing. In Y2, teachers questioned children about the properties of shapes, the properties of materials, place value, Venn diagrams and the formation of letters.

Teachers questioned children during the middle of lessons to assess them. At times, during the middle of maths lessons, when children had completed one worksheet and were about to move on to another sheet, teachers would give spot questions on the content of the new sheet to judge whether the child had enough understanding to proceed. For example, a Y6 teacher checked that two children knew the number of playing cards in a pack, the number and names of cards in each suit, before she set them to work on the particular probability problem.

Often, when teachers were commanding the attention of the whole class at the end of a lesson, they would ask a set of questions (closed, requiring correct short or more explanatory answers) of the whole group, taking answers from those who volunteered. The purpose behind this appeared to be to estimate how much had been 'generally' taken in. At other times, at the end of lessons, teachers of both age groups would pick on individuals or give every child a question, for example giving 'quick-fire sums' to check what they had learned. In a Y2 classroom, the teacher ended the maths session with a quick quiz game: she asked each child a multiplication question pitched at their own ability level to assess what they had gained from the teaching. Another Y2 teacher asked each individual in a group of similar ability how they had made 20p from a set of coins. A third example was when a Y2 teacher quizzed individuals about the functions of different maths signs, checking that they had understood.

Oral testing was also used in the type of lesson which had no clear beginning, middle or end, but in which children just 'got on' with some routine work. In three of our Y6 classrooms children worked at their own pace for whole lessons through a series of graded maths workcards. When a child had completed a card in their individual programme, teachers invariably gave a brief oral test on the maths learned on that card to judge whether the child had grasped the main points and had been using appropriate strategies. Some questions were closed and quiz-like, '*How many degrees are there in a triangle?*' and others were more probing – requiring more than a one-word explanation from the child, '*Can you tell me the difference between a prism and a pyramid?*'; '*If you want to construct a box what do you do?*'. Both types of questions were used to confirm that a child had learned particular things from working independently.

Oral testing of individuals clearly differed from oral testing in the whole-class context, mainly in that questions were tailored to what individuals were working on. Teachers often took the opportunity of 'homing in' on individuals while children were set to activities. At times we were able to observe those interactions and see where oral testing fitted into the dialogue between teacher and pupil. A common sequence was when a teacher had noticed a child's mistakes in punctuation. The teacher might read the child's work, pausing to indicate where a full stop was needed, then test: '*What do we need here?*'. Whatever the child's response, the teacher would always give feedback. This was usually followed by '*What comes after a full stop?*'. Once again whatever the child's response, the teacher would always give feedback. So in this case the sequence was assessment (checking work) – teaching – assessment (oral testing) – feedback.

For some teachers oral testing was closely associated with another assessment strategy. At the beginning of lessons when teachers were engaging the whole class in a kind of revision quiz to judge what they had retained from a previous lesson, they explained they would also be 'making a mental note' about children who appeared not to know and to require more input. If a number of children seemed to be having difficulties, the teacher might repeat the lesson. As a Y6 teacher explained: '*I use this to find out where they are because they are all at different places . . . and I can bulk teach what it is [they don't seem to know]*'. In this context one assessment strategy (oral testing) was used almost synonymously with another (making a mental assessment note), leading to repeating teaching (relaying knowledge/remodelling something).

- *'Delving'*

As with oral testing, 'delving' was not specified by teachers. They simply called it questioning. One Y2 teacher explained how she uses *'a kind of open-ended questioning where it isn't a yes or no answer'*. She went on to say *'We need to delve a bit deeper than that as far as their understanding is concerned'*. Hence, this type of questioning which involves probing a child's thinking and learning strategies through a range of open and closed questions, we named 'delving'. It was described by other teachers of both age groups. For example, a Y6 teacher explained: *'It's probably something like "How did you actually arrive at that?" Yes. "How did you get there"?'*. 'Delving' was not very often observed, possibly because classes were large (25–30 children); teachers for the most part tried to interact with as many children as possible in a lesson and therefore did not spend lengthy periods of time with individuals. We noticed that 'delving' was part of a teacher's overall personal style (at least three Y2 and five Y6 teachers used it regularly).

The function of 'delving' appeared to be diagnostic – an analysis of learning in order to gain understanding and aid future planning. Delving could be triggered by a child's constant mistakes, or indeed success, or simply by the teacher's curiosity about a child's methods. 'Delving' was always directed at an individual and, when observed, it was a constructive activity: 'delving' never became grilling, pumping or cross-examining. Its purpose was to help children in the end and not to 'test' them.

In the words of one Y6 teacher:

> They might be using some complex method in order to arrive at the correct answer and that's what I'm looking for because then, if I feel this is a very slow way, I might say 'Can I show you one way that I know?'

The relationship implied here among teaching, assessment and feedback is sequential: assessment (delving) – assessment (getting a child to demonstrate) – descriptive feedback (specifying a better way of doing something) – teaching (relaying knowledge/demonstrating).

One Y2 teacher explained: *'I try to discover what's preventing the learning happening'* and although 'delving' was usually used for this reason, a teacher might equally probe to assess why a child was coping easily, and often the teacher used a child's successful system or method as an exemplar for the rest of the class.

Delving was an assessment strategy most commonly observed in maths but also in science; teachers usually made use of it when they were working with individuals or with groups engaged on collaborative tasks.

One Y2 teacher described using this kind of questioning to find out *'what their thinking has been behind problem solving'*. Having taught her seven year olds for the first time about the purpose of the key on a diagram, she focused on a group of eight doing a worksheet and asked each child probing questions to determine how they had reached an answer and whether they had been using the key to find their answers. In another Y2 classroom, children were encouraged to design their own 'nets' for 3D shapes. When some of the nets did not work, the teacher asked the children to open them out and look carefully and she probed about the layout and the accuracy of the edges until children could make suggestions about where they had gone wrong. In a Y6 classroom, the children were asked to look at sums and choose the correct answer from a set of three, using fast checking techniques they had just learned. As the teacher circulated while children were working through some examples, he delved to find out how individuals had reached answers, asking for example: *'Why did you decide to put that?'*, *'What made you do that?'*, *'So what you did there was to . . . ?'*, *'Why did you choose that method?'*. (Note that the teacher's tone of voice was not at all hectoring – rather, he was asking for information in an interested and supportive way.)

In a remarkable instance, at the end of a Y6 science lesson, 'delving' was not the prerogative of the teacher. Groups had been doing various sinking and floating experiments, looking at the properties of different materials. In a plenary session, when groups expressed their difficulties the other children immediately began to ask questions such as *'Did you try so-and-so?'*, *'Had you thought about . . . ?'*.

We looked at the place of 'delving' in teacher–pupil interactions where the focus was on helping children to overcome misunderstandings in maths. A number of other strategies clustered around 'delving' in this context. A teacher would normally have assessed work in advance and have the child's worked examples in front of her. The interaction with the child would involve reference to the examples, questioning about how the child had got to the answers, getting the child to demonstrate their method, more questioning, specifying a better way of doing something, modelling, observing the child doing, more questioning and giving feedback on the child's new performance. The sequence in these interactions was assessment, feedback, teaching, assessment, feedback; it is difficult, however, to portray the complexity of these interactions.

e) Getting a child to demonstrate

In interview, four Y6 and five Y2 teachers described an assessment strategy of '*getting the child to do something for you*'. This strategy could be used directly, for example, getting children to go through the methods they had used to arrive at a solution or less directly, maybe by getting children to show another child how to do something or getting children to play a game, while the teacher watched.

One function of this approach was to judge whether children were going astray in their learning strategies, another was to confirm that they had learned something, another was '*just to see*' what they could do and another was to judge whether children could apply what they had learned to a problem solving operation.

Getting children to demonstrate was used as an assessment strategy in maths and English. It was used privately with individuals and publicly in whole-class situations. It was used so that teachers could assess what one child was able to do and it was used so that teachers could get a picture of general understanding.

When a teacher wanted to judge whether children were going astray in their learning strategies, they would usually work individually with the child. In maths, when children had made mistakes teachers, in order to diagnose error, often asked them to demonstrate how they had been doing the work. For example, a Y2 boy could not master the making of a cube so the teacher told him to '*take it apart and show me how you made it*'. We observed instances of teachers (of both age groups) watching as children demonstrated their subtraction strategies, their use of calculators, and their use of rulers and other measuring instruments. A teacher might however choose to assess a child's maths knowledge publicly, for example by getting the child to recite multiplication tables in front of the class.

In reading comprehension lessons in Y6, we observed three teachers ask individuals to read aloud questions which they had wrongly answered, in an attempt to understand if misreading had been instrumental in the child's misunderstanding. In Y2 classrooms we observed teachers asking children to form letters ('*Can I see you doing one of these, please?*') to diagnose why handwriting was poorly formed. Spelling aloud, reading aloud and acting were all means of getting children to demonstrate what they could do and so offered an opportunity for assessment.

When a teacher wanted to assess the use and application of something learned they might present a group with a challenge. For example, in maths teachers might ask children to play games to show how well they had understood and could apply learning (e.g. play 'Snakes and Ladders' which involves counting on and counting back). For assessment purposes the teacher would closely observe the children's strategies.

In whole-class teaching situations, we observed teachers assessing what the majority knew by getting them to do something. For example a Y2 teacher gave each child a cardboard clock with moving hands and asked them to show various times, holding up their answers so that she could judge the general understanding. In another Y2 class, the teacher asked all the children to use their fingers to show how tall a 1cm ball would be. This allowed her to assess instantly those who could see the difference between 'tall' and 'wide' and those who could not.

Getting children to demonstrate was usually accompanied by observing or, in some cases, 'delving'; then followed teacher demonstration and specifying a better way of doing something. Here assessment was followed by teaching/descriptive feedback.

Teachers of both age groups used 'getting children to demonstrate'. Infant teachers were more likely to make use of whole-class teaching situations than junior teachers, while teachers of both age groups got individual children to demonstrate in order to evaluate the methods they were using.

f) Checking

Both Y6 and Y2 teachers described how they went round checking when children had begun on activities. Checking meant '*assessing children as they are doing it – watching them*' or briefly examining children's efforts against particular criteria they had in mind and making an instant judgement about whether children were on the right lines. In this way checking was different from observing 'on the hoof' in that teachers knew what they were looking for.

The point of checking was to see if children were applying what had just been taught or asked for; in the words of one teacher: '*Looking for all those things I have already covered – checking on capitals and full stops, checking on spellings*'. Other teachers reported checking on whether children were correctly applying a number operation, whether they were using mathematical instruments correctly, whether they were presenting work in the way the teacher had asked for.

Checking was carried out at the point in the lesson when children were engaged in activities; teachers who focused their teaching on one group during the middle part of lessons did less checking on the whole class, but did more checking on the work of this one group. 'Checking' was common in all subjects and in most lessons, except those in which the teacher addressed the whole class for the whole of the time. In our observations teachers rarely stood back and relaxed when the children were working!

Checking allowed teachers to 'gauge the level' of individual or group progress on a task (see later section) and could, depending on the child's/children's success, be followed by any strategy from the wide repertoire of teaching, assessment and feedback. For example checking could be followed by:

- oral testing (punctuation exercises): 'What should you have started your sentences with?';

- questioning to promote thinking (science group work): 'Where are you going to drop the balls from? On to what?';

- reminding or re-demonstrating (science group work): Teacher showed the group how to hold a measuring tape in such a way as to make an accurate measurement;

- providing support materials (writing an opening paragraph): Teacher gave a child a spelling tips book;

- giving evaluative feedback (most lessons, all subjects): 'Good – you have made a good start';

- specifying a better way of doing something (making a space for 'work-ings out' in maths): 'If you use your ruler, you'll get a straighter margin'.

'Checking' could, of course be followed by no teaching or feedback, when the teacher, having ascertained a child was working appropriately, simply moved on to the next child. At times teachers would return to the same child checking for improvement after input had been given. As with observing, 'checking' could lead the teacher to stop the class and relay some teaching point she had picked up on while circulating.

Checking was a very common strategy and was used extensively by teachers of both age groups. As more Y2 than Y6 teachers focused attention on one group when children were set to task, they were less likely than Y6 to check on the whole class during lessons, although they carried out intensive checking on groups.

g) Listening

Over half the teachers explained that they used listening as an assessment technique. Although they did listen to children's answers to oral testing questions of course, listening came more into its own as an assessment strategy when teachers considered children's answers to more exploratory/open-ended questions or when teachers engaged in 'delving'. When teachers used 'delving' in maths, listening helped them make a judgement on the appropriateness of a child's methods. When teachers used open-ended questioning in science, listening helped them assess what a child knew or understood. Two teachers explained that they might ask a child to explain something to another child and, by listening to the child's explanation, use the occasion to make an assessment of the child-teacher's understanding. However, listening was described and used as a strategy most in the assessment of speaking and listening, and reading. We observed occasions in 11 infant classrooms when teachers listened to individuals reading. As teachers listened to a child read, they assessed the child's fluency and ability to read with expression. They used open-ended questions and listened carefully to the child's answers to assess a child's ability to predict what might happen next and/or what the author might have implied in certain passages.

In three instances, we could see that teachers were listening carefully in order to assess a child's ability to speak in front of the class, whether by reporting on an activity they had done or giving a verbal self-assessment of their year's work.

The use of listening as strategy to find out what children knew and understood was common in at least four Y6 teachers' science lessons, exemplified in a Y6 class when children were investigating soil in pairs. The activity prompted the teacher to ask open-ended questions depending on what children found in their own particular mound of soil. For example, when a leaf skeleton was unearthed the teacher asked – '. . . and what do you think happened here? . . .'. When a worm crawled out the teacher asked 'Is there anything surprising about this?'. When a boy found some sand, the teacher asked 'What makes you decide that it's sand?'. Overall, by carefully listening to the conceptualisation in children's answers the teacher gained insights into how they were thinking, what they knew and whether they were using close observation and evidence.

Teachers of both age groups used listening as an assessment technique. In our observations Y2 were seen to use it alongside open-ended questioning in reading and Y6 alongside exploratory questions in science and as a result of 'delving' in maths.

h) Eavesdropping – a covert listening strategy

Eavesdropping was an indirect assessment strategy a few teachers referred to, but it was a strategy that we observed more widely. Eavesdropping went on while children were working on activities – teachers would stand near a group and listen in to the group's discussion, brainstorming or task planning. Teachers of both age groups used eavesdropping in all subject contexts.

Eavesdropping was used to assess how children were attacking a given task, e.g. their use of collaborative skills or the roles children adopted in a design-and-make task. Teachers might use eavesdropping to see how children were using information they had been given through teaching, e.g. whether children were using scientific vocabulary and terminology when designing a fair test (Y6); whether pairs were using some of the suggestions given in the teacher's introduction to a poetry lesson (Y2). Eavesdropping was also part of planned, focused observation for assessment, and we witnessed a specific example of this when a Y2 teacher moved round the class, listening in to pairs reading to each other, taking notes on their collaborative behaviour and on individuals' reading strategies. In teacher–pupil interaction, *listening* was usually preceded by questioning while *eavesdropping* was preceded by relaying knowledge or relaying learning strategies.

i) Marking

When asked which assessment strategies they used, a quarter of Y6 and a few Y2 teachers volunteered marking. They reported reading what children had written, amending spellings and punctuation or putting ticks and crosses on maths and English work.

Although the teachers mentioned the feedback function of marking (telling children they were right or wrong) they described how for them the very act of marking helped them to evaluate children's attainment or learning strategies. Marking stimulated the analysis of children's work as well as reflection: recurring errors became obvious, sometimes errors of the same type, which gave teachers an idea of what a child might be doing wrong. (See also 'working out why a child has or has not achieved'.)

Teachers marked work in maths, science and writing. Sometimes they marked work as they circulated while children were doing tasks. Ticks and crosses were usually followed by verbal feedback, usually explaining why an answer was correct or wrong. At other times teachers marked work at home. On these occasions the reflections generated by marking would prompt teachers (mainly Y6) to write notes to children, telling them what they had or had not achieved. (See Chapter 5 for details of written feedback).

j) Making a mental assessment note

In interview two Y2 teachers constantly referred to 'making a mental note' and this led us to search the data for other references to this strategy. It transpired that other teachers (of both age groups) described noting, logging and committing to memory a judgment made of a child or a child's knowledge, skills, understanding or learning strategies. These judgments were described as 'unconscious-type assessments' and came from sudden flashes of insight gained from interaction with the child or the child's work. To quote one Y2 teacher:

> As I go along I suppose every time a child answers, I'm sure that unconsciously I am making some assessment of where the child is at.

A teacher might make a mental note about a child's or a group's grasp of something taught. Similarly, a teacher might note a child's appropriate or inappropriate learning strategy. However, mental notes were not only made about a child's progress but also about a child's enthusiasm for learning or elements of a child's personality that had a bearing on learning style. Mental notes served as an *aide mémoire* and sometimes stimulated teacher intervention, not at the point of making the note but usually some time later for example, at the next lesson on a topic. The point about a mental note was that it was there as a reminder, a kind of directive to themselves about future teaching.

A whole store of mental notes helped teachers to build up an overall picture of the child and its learning and this could be useful when teachers were giving verbal feedback or writing feedback on work and when they were writing reports.

Teachers made mental notes all the time in every subject and in every context. Making mental notes was another element in what teachers kept describing as 'assessing all the time'. They explained that they were logging and 'clocking' things about children throughout every stage of every lesson. For example, a Y2 teacher explained that during a lesson when children had been practising and consolidating the idea of place value she had noted the children who still did not seem to be achieving and would need some further input.

A Y2 teacher recounted how marking or reading work can generate sudden understanding and a personal memo about future action. She explained:

> When I look back (over a child's books) I think to myself 'blimey, I've said that lots of times, this child's obviously still not got full stops'. She makes a mental note: 'He hasn't actually got that yet, he's still higgledy-piggledy. Right this child needs extra work on that'. Then she intervenes, asking the child to practise, while constantly reminding him: 'don't forget to put your full stops in'.

It could be that repeated reminders may be given to particular children as a result of mental notes as much as a result of written marking.

After a series of lessons on the same topic, a teacher might draw on mental notes to decide what to teach next. Mental notes are called up during the period of reflection after a school day, as a Y2 teacher explained:

> I think you have to say to yourself sometimes – OK, we did that, most of them got it, but some of them didn't. . . .

As with gauging the level, making a mental note played a hidden part in pupil–teacher interactions and similarly its outcome was usually teaching, whether giving a child further information, modelling or demonstrating or directing to further practise.

k) Gauging the level

'Gauging the level' was a mental activity, described by one teacher as 'actually making some sort of judgment on where a child is in terms of progress'. In daily teaching, gauging the level was synonymous with what teachers described as 'assessing all the time'. As an assessment strategy, gauging the level involved judging the degree of progress made either by individuals or by a proportion of the whole class. In another sense, however, gauging the level of a child was described (by a few teachers) in relation to assessing a child against the NC programmes of study.

Gauging the level had a number of functions; it could be part of 'feeling the way through' teaching and used to help teachers build their input. One Y2 teacher explained that she gauges the level of understanding of the majority of the class while she is teaching, mainly through children's answers to open questions, through children's queries

and through children's voluntary contributions. Based on her judgement, she decides how to pitch her teaching somewhere between
'*challenge and threat*'. In this sense, children's responses to questions
and their unsolicited contributions are used to gauge the general level
of understanding of a class.

Teachers listened to children's offerings, turned them over in their
minds and made minute-to-minute judgments about what to do next
(i.e. immediately). Describing how '*gauging the level*' helped them build
their input, teachers explained:

> I might have said something and the kids are fully aware of it, more aware
> than I thought, so I think, quickly, I've got to move on. Sometimes it is
> thinking on your feet and making those snappy decisions. (Y6)

> As I am teaching I might introduce more questions because I am listen-
> ing to what the children are giving me. (Y2)

Gauging the level was a means to '*pitching*' teaching appropriately.

> As you start to speak, you must respond to how the children take on the
> ideas you are putting forward. If it is quite clear that the ideas are going
> over their heads or are inappropriate to their needs, then you have got to
> keep on either moving backwards, maybe simplifying or rephrasing things,
> or going off in a slightly different direction. (Y6)

In relation to individual children, teachers used '*gauging the level*' to
get a picture of the child's stage in understanding a current task ('*where
they actually seem to be at this minute in response to the task*') so that a
decision could be made about whether to intervene or allow the child
to continue. In this way 'gauging the level' went alongside 'checking'
and marking work 'on the hoof'.

Teachers used gauging the level as an assessment strategy in all
subjects and in a variety of contexts – in classrooms while interacting
with children, and out of school when children were not present.
To gauge the level of progress being made during a lesson, teachers
frequently checked on individual children to monitor their progress in
relation to the learning objectives of the lesson. If misunderstandings
were noticed, teachers gave some kind of feedback (for example, telling
children they were right or wrong) and then some input or intervention
(for example, further explaining, demonstrating, modelling or directing
a child to further practise.) In the case of one observed maths lesson

where children were being introduced to co-ordinates, a teacher circulated, checked work for understanding, gave some children a GOT IT stamp if he judged that their understanding met his learning objectives and questioned (delved) other children to clear up misunderstandings.

In relation to collaborative group work on 'good story starts', one Y6 teacher described how eavesdropping helped her to gauge the level of the thinking of one group:

> *I could see the sort of direction their thoughts as a group were going and . . . they were having a little bit of difficulty starting [to brainstorm] . . .*

Teachers reported gauging the level of *general* understanding at the end of a lesson. One Y6 teacher described how, to gauge progress during the plenary, she would use oral testing and get children to demonstrate the science they had learned:

> *. . . when you want to make sure that they understand the content of what you intended them to learn . . . {you ask} 'Do they understand what a balanced force is? Can they give me examples before we go?'.*

After a lesson had finished, a teacher might reflect on what had been learned generally across the group and mull over any future action. For example, one Y2 teacher, having come out of a 'fast track' maths group, reported:

> *I could sense that they weren't exactly sure with the numbers that they were working with so I made a mental note to inform the other teachers.*

Finally, teachers described gauging the level from scrutinising work. They assessed individual pieces of writing completed during the term and they assessed samples of individual children's work at the *end* of a term/year, gauging the level of a child in terms of National Assessment levels. In the words of another Y6 teacher:

> *Depending on the samples you have done throughout the year, you would match the child to which box [level] they belong – best fit. That's what I use to get my TA from, by using the NC levels.*

Gauging the level was a significant strategy and played an important (if hidden) part in pupil–teacher interactions. It was the link between what the teacher had learned from various assessment techniques (questioning, getting a child to demonstrate, checking the work of the class) and what she decided to do next *vis-à-vis* teaching (e.g. giving more explanation, modelling, re-demonstrating, relaying new knowledge, questioning to promote thinking). As such it was really an evaluation, or summing up, of information.

l) Working out why a child has or has not achieved

Teachers did not describe this as an assessment strategy. However, it came through in their conversations and in our observations. In the words of one Y6 teacher: '*I have to look in more detail and more critically at what is going on . . . I have to look in a more considered way at the children's work*'. So the strategy was linked somewhat to marking in that marking stimulated reflection on recurring errors of the same type, giving teachers an idea of what a child might be doing wrong.

A Y2 teacher explained: '*I work on a one-to-one basis, trying to talk through where the problem lies*'. So the strategy was linked also to delving, or getting a child to demonstrate – both were ways in which teachers tried to assess what was amiss or successful in a child's methods or theorising. But mainly it was a process of trial and error on behalf of the teachers who struggled to find out ways in which they could connect with and understand children's learning strategies. As with gauging the level, this is an evaluation activity. The function was mainly to try to diagnose where a child was going wrong and so to decide on appropriate teaching strategies. In the words of another Y6 teacher: '*It's for me to learn what I need to do for that child to succeed*'. It was a strategy used more by teachers who had a reflective style.

To summarise, the teachers used a wide repertoire of assessment strategies:

- using other teachers' records;
- testing;
- observing;
- questioning – oral testing;
- questioning – delving;
- getting a child to demonstrate;
- checking;
- listening;
- eavesdropping;
- marking;

- making a mental assessment note;
- gauging the level – assessing general level of understanding;
- gauging the level – judging progress;
- gauging the level – looking at a range of work to make a summative judgement; and
- working out why a child has or has not achieved.

These can be grouped in the following ways:

- **Those which involve teacher–pupil interaction**
  Testing
  Questioning – oral testing
  Questioning – delving
  Getting a child to demonstrate
- **Those which involve the teacher in watching and listening**
  Observing
  Checking
  Listening
  Eavesdropping
- **Those which involve the teacher in 'mentally' considering the evidence**
  Using other teachers' records
  Marking
  Making a mental assessment note
  Gauging the level – assessing general level of understanding
  Gauging the level – judging progress
  Gauging the level – looking at range of work to make a summative judgement
  Working out why a child has or has not achieved

Overall, some strategies appeared to be used MORE to assess a child's *knowledge and understanding* while others were used MORE to assess a child's *learning strategies*. Some strategies spanned both uses. (See Figure 4.1.)

Overall, we found that Y2 and Y6 teachers coincided more in their assessment practice than they differed. Teachers of both age groups used observing, oral testing, getting a child to demonstrate, marking, listening, making mental assessment notes and working out why a child has or has not achieved in the same ways and in the same contexts. Teachers of both age groups described the process of 'gauging the level'

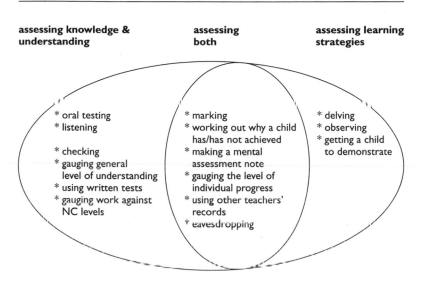

| assessing knowledge &
understanding | assessing
both | assessing learning
strategies |

* oral testing
* listening

* checking
* gauging general
  level of understanding
* using written tests
* gauging work against
  NC levels

* marking
* working out why a child
  has/has not achieved
* making a mental
  assessment note
* gauging the level of
  individual progress
* using other teachers'
  records
* eavesdropping

* delving
* observing
* getting a child
  to demonstrate

Figure 4.1 Assessment strategies

of general understanding in the class, of individual progress and of samples of work.

We found that Y6 teachers were more likely to use standardised tests than Y2 teachers and in general to do more testing; that 'delving', although used by both Y2 and Y6 teachers was observed most often in Y6 maths lessons. More Y2 than Y6 teachers used a lesson pattern involving focused attention on one group when children were set to task. This resulted in some Y2 teachers being less likely to check on the whole class during pupil activities, but more likely to carry out intensive checking on one group.

Three-quarters of the heads had suggested that assessment strategies were likely to be different for different subjects, suggesting: maths by written tests, writing by scrutinising a piece of unaided writing against SAT criteria, reading by listening and discussing and science by observation. Our analysis suggests that there *were* some strategies favoured in different subjects or aspects of those subjects, but there were also many assessment strategies used in all core subjects, and in some cases all aspects (or ATs) of core subjects, as Table 4.1 shows.

Table 4.1 Analysis of favoured assessment strategies

Assessment strategy	Chiefly used to assess:
• **Using other teachers' records**	All core subjects
• **Using written tests**	
(standardised)	All aspects of English and maths
(own tests/tasks)	Most aspects of all core subjects
• **Observing**	
('noticing')	All core subjects
(watching and listening)	Speaking and listening
	Experimental and investigative maths and science
• **Questioning**	
(oral testing)	All core subjects
(delving)	Number operations and investigative science
• **Getting a child to**	Reading, handwriting
demonstrate	Space and measures in maths and science
• **Checking**	Writing, all maths, all science
• **Marking**	All written aspects of all core subjects
• **Listening**	Reading
	Experimental and investigative science
• **Eavesdropping**	Speaking and listening in groups
	Experimental and investigative maths and science in groups
• **Gauging the level**	
(general level of understanding)	All aspects of all core subjects
(judging progress)	All aspects of all core subjects
(against NC levels)	All written aspects of all core subjects
• **Making a mental assessment note**	All aspects of all core subjects
• **Working out why a child has or hasn't achieved**	Writing, reading comprehension and maths (all aspects)

We now turn to the feedback strategies teachers used and told us about.

Chapter 5

Feedback

INTRODUCTION

The previous chapter described strategies teachers use to make their informal assessments. In Chapter 1 we outlined how teachers can use their formative assessments about children's learning and understanding to improve the learning process. One way that they do this is by giving feedback to the learner directly about what is going well or done well, what is not right, and how it can be improved.

In this chapter we examine the feedback strategies teachers used in order to give feedback directly to children. We defined a feedback strategy as one where the teacher is

> *imparting directly a judgement of a child, a child's strategies and skills, or a child's attainment (often in relation to goals) and giving information about the judgement.*

From our research, we found out that teachers used feedback strategies in a range of ways: they presented their judgements and gave information about the judgements, to different audiences, in different forms and for different purposes.

Feedback was given:

- to individuals;
- to pairs and groups; or
- to the whole class.

Feedback could be:

- verbal;
- non-verbal;
- written; or
- written and verbal at the same time.

The content of the feedback itself fell into two broad categories:

- feedback could be evaluative, that is judgmental, with implicit or explicit use of norms and could be positive or negative.

Or

- feedback could be descriptive, with specific reference to the child's actual achievement or competence and could relate to either achievement or improvement.

These categories were drawn out by Tunstall and Gipps (1996, Chapter 1), who developed a classification or typology of formative assessment feedback. In the current research, we were able to use Tunstall and Gipps' classification as a framework and then to develop it further. Their typology is shown in Table 5.1 at the end of this chapter.

In this chapter, first, we report comments made by headteachers and teachers about feedback generally. The purpose of presenting these comments is to see what teachers and headteachers actually understand by 'feedback'. Then we describe different feedback strategies; the nature and function of each feedback strategy is described, using evidence taken from our observations and from teachers' own accounts to us in interview.

The feedback strategies that we explore are the following:

Evaluative:
- **giving rewards and punishments;**
- **expressing approval and disapproval.**

Descriptive:
- **telling children they are right or wrong;**
- **describing why an answer is correct;**
- **telling children what they have and have not achieved;**
- **specifying or implying a better way of doing something; and**
- **getting children to suggest ways they can improve.**

GENERAL COMMENTS ABOUT FEEDBACK

Several headteachers told us that feedback was crucial and that better teachers gave more feedback. Some said that the importance of feedback was reflected in their school marking policy. A few of these described how the policy encouraged teachers to plan time dedicated to giving feedback, for example, during the lunch break when teachers could see children in smaller groups or one to one.

Some teachers and headteachers felt that verbal, immediate feedback was the most useful for the child's learning, particularly for younger children. Teachers stressed, though, that the way in which feedback was given was vital; that is, it was very important how they couched the wording or implication of their feedback. In particular, they needed to make criticisms or give negative feedback very sensitively. Teachers emphasised the importance of feedback being positive. There was some feeling that this applied especially in Y2. One Y2 teacher explained,

> You don't go and say, 'Oh, you are doing it wrong', you always try and look for the way around to make it into a positive situation, because you could put them off.

One way of remaining positive in feedback, was by making comments only on specific and limited aspects of work so that the feedback did not appear too daunting. One Y2 teacher, for example, told us that she informed children at the start of a writing lesson that she was concentrating on spelling, or sentences, and then she only gave feedback in the one area on that occasion.

At the same time, however, teachers told us that feedback must be honest. One Y2 teacher expressed this,

> You can't constantly tell children things are wonderful when they aren't, because they don't actually learn anything.

Another important aspect of feedback was that different children were receptive to different presentations and different types of feedback. The teacher had to assess which presentation and which type of feedback would be most useful to each individual child. One Y6 teacher explained,

> I have got a couple of boys who respond really well to me being really sarcastic . . . whereas I've got another couple of girls, if I did that to them, they are going to burst into tears.

Evaluative feedback

a) Giving rewards and punishments

When teachers gave a reward or punishment, they rarely made explicit reference to the child's particular learning achievement or lack of achievement. The giving of rewards and punishments was therefore a form of evaluative feedback. Rewards and punishments were given to individuals rather than to pairs, groups, or the whole class. The strategy could be verbal, non-verbal or written.

As rewards on written work, Y2 and Y6 teachers drew or stamped smiley faces, gave stickers or other stamps, stars, merits or house points. They might give these rewards as they praised the child in interaction. Other rewards included being clapped by the rest of the class, being invited to write on the blackboard, being awarded extra time on the computer or CD ROM or being allowed to work alone. A couple of headteachers described how children would be asked to show particularly good work to other members of staff or the head. Others talked of the value of sharing an individual's good work with other children, for example, in a 'praise and share' assembly.

Punishments consisted of the withholding of rewards in many cases, or even the removal of rewards such as a deduction of house points. One teacher gave un-smiley faces. Children were moved away from friends, and told to work through their lunch time or do extra homework, if they were not working efficiently. In one case, a Y6 boy was sent down to compare his work with that of Y2 children, and another teacher tore up work that was not worthy of the child. These two examples were rare and since they rely on shaming children we could not agree that they are part of 'good practice'.

Rewards were used to motivate children in the sense of encouraging them to keep learning and keep trying, to think, 'I've done well here'. Rewards could raise children's self-esteem and so spur them on. A Y6 teacher described how,

> The stars abound in science books because they really take a pride in them and they enjoy it.

She explained,

> I work for a salary, they should be able to work for a star or something, a treat.

There were no indications that rewards and punishments were used more in one particular subject. Our data indicate that rewards played a more important role in Y2 than in Y6, perhaps because some teachers felt that children's self-esteem and confidence needed more boosting at the earlier age.

b) Expressing approval and disapproval

Teachers expressed approval saying, for example, 'Well done', 'Good boy/girl', 'Brilliant'. Expressions of disapproval included such criticisms as 'Don't talk rubbish!' As with other feedback strategies, the strategy of expressing approval and disapproval could be verbal, non-verbal or written. Non-verbal strategies of expressing approval included the teacher nodding, making eye contact, smiling, laughing, putting an arm around or patting the child and taking on a mild manner in order to be approachable. Non-verbal means of expressing disapproval included pulling faces, staring hard, clicking fingers or making disapproving noises. Verbal expressions of approval or disapproval sometimes accompanied non-verbal expressions. Sometimes rewards and punishments accompanied these. For example, one Y2 teacher who smiled at a child who had done well, stuck a 'Well done' sticker to her cardigan and praised her verbally as she did so.

The expression of approval and disapproval was a form of evaluative feedback in that often its purpose was to show approval or disapproval of the child him or herself, rather than his or her achievement. For example, we observed teachers thanking a child or expressing their own pleasure, saying, 'Well done, I'm very pleased with you'. Sometimes, the teacher implied that she felt that work was 'Excellent' or 'Disappointing', but without relating this evaluation to specified achievement criteria.

Approval and disapproval could be expressed to individuals, pairs or groups, or the whole class. Teachers sometimes fed back to the whole class whether they had done well or not. They believed that approving or disapproving feedback given to one individual in front of the rest of the class, could inspire the other children to do better or urge them to avoid undesirable behaviour.

The vast majority of verbal expressions of approval were in the form of praise phrases. Teachers offered praise for correct answers, for good work, for using a good method, for effort and for independent thinking. Several teachers gave praise by gender, for example, saying, 'Good boy' or 'Good girl'. Disapproval was most commonly expressed in relation to behaviour, although this was often learning behaviour. For example, teachers expressed disapproval when children argued, were not listening, or were not concentrating.

An indirect strategy for showing disapproval was when teachers dismissed or ignored a child's contribution on purpose. For example, in a 'carpet' session, if a child called out an answer, the teacher chose to ignore it. It generally applied to the individual rather than groups or the whole class, although in a whole-class setting, some teachers deliberately asked for the contributions of the weakest or most timid learners in their classes to the *exclusion* of others. One teacher actually told a stronger learner to stop responding, in order to let a weaker learner make her point. These examples show that there could also be occasions when the use of this strategy was not negative.

In other cases, however, dismissal of a child's contribution strongly implied disapproval, as when teachers became tired of waiting for a child's answer, or ignored incorrect answers and turned to ask someone else. Others told the child he or she was wrong and then turned to someone else. In one case we observed, a child began talking about food when the topic of conversation was clothes, so the teacher responded with '*Hang on, we're talking about clothes*'. In another case, the teacher cut short a child who was talking for too long. We observed two teachers who dismissed a child's answer because someone else had already given it.

Several teachers and headteachers considered the expression of approval to be a means of showing the child that he or she was valued, and of increasing children's self-esteem and so their confidence about being good learners. Verbal and non-verbal expressions of approval functioned, for many teachers, to encourage children to:

• continue working;
• move on to the next stage of their work;
• want to contribute in class;
• be willing to find things out;
• take risks; or
• work independently.

One teacher commented that, '. . . *the more motivated the child the easier it is to get that child to want to learn for itself*'. This feedback strategy was paralleled by teaching strategies which were also used to motivate children. Although we might expect Y2 teachers to stress the need for expressions of approval more than Y6 teachers, our data did not support this. Teachers from Y2 and Y6 stressed the importance of giving negative as well as positive feedback, although a few teachers felt that younger children needed less negative feedback than older children. One Y6 teacher admitted she would sometimes be honest and say it was '*a really dreadful piece of work*'. Negative feedback served to make a future occurrence less likely. In a whole-class setting, for example, one teacher asked all the class a question. When only three hands went up, she looked disapproving. This encouraged more children to put up their hands after the subsequent question.

Because the function was motivation towards achievement rather than specific achievement itself, the evaluative nature of this type of feedback was not surprising. Several teachers, however, recognised that evaluative feedback which showed their approval or disapproval needed to be accompanied by descriptive feedback which explained why an answer was right or good or how it might be improved. For example, one teacher said,

> . . . *there is no point in you praising a child, patronising them and saying this is wonderful, this is good, all the time, when really and truly they don't know what's good about whatever it is, they haven't been given any pointers or tips of how to improve* . . .

The use of this feedback strategy was not limited to a particular lesson type or stage in the lesson since teachers saw motivating (through approval) and controlling children (through disapproval) as of ongoing usefulness. One unique context in which teachers expressed approval was, however, creative writing in children's exercise books. When we surveyed pieces of creative writing, we found that sometimes teachers gave personal comments about the contents of a child's story as their only form of feedback, presumably implying approval or disapproval but not conveying a sense of what was good or less good about the story. For example, we saw: '*I hope you had a good time at the cliffs*', '*He sounds very strange*' and '*Oh dear, it sounds too scary for me*'.

Descriptive feedback

c) Telling children they are right or wrong

The first stage towards describing to a pupil what is good or less good about his or her achievement may involve the teacher feeding back to the child whether a response is right or wrong. Telling a child that he or she has a right answer is feedback itself, with an implication that the particular area in which the child has been right is now mastered. Telling a child that he or she has a wrong answer is feedback that implies that the child should look again at the task, although through this strategy the nature of the improvement is not described.

Our research showed that a simple way of telling children they were wrong, was for the teacher to say 'No', and perhaps to turn to someone else for the right answer. Teachers used this strategy with individuals, rather than with groups or the whole class, although one Y2 teacher was heard to tell the whole class, '*You always, always stumble on this one*' in the context of a mathematics concept. Teachers could feed back to children that they were wrong by demonstrating themselves: one teacher acted on a child's suggestions for using a measuring scale, already knowing they were incorrect, to allow the child to see for herself that they would not work.

On written work, teachers might indicate an incorrect response with a cross, dot or underlining, or an empty box where the child could write the correct answer. One Y2 teacher we observed rubbed out children's incorrect answers in their exercise books. In all subjects we observed, crosses to indicate a wrong answer were less common than ticks to indicate a correct one. Some Y2 teachers put ticks but never crosses on work.

Sometimes teachers fed back that an answer was incorrect by putting a question to the child, either repeating an original question or posing a new one. For example, one Y6 teacher read out a limerick and asked the class to find a word to rhyme with '*Bengal*'; one child said, '*party*', and the teacher did not say '*No*' but asked him why he said party and then asked what other rhymes were in the poem. We observed that some teachers invited the child to reread a question or redo his or her own answer, as their way to show the child that he or she was wrong. On one child's book was written '*What does that say?*' as an indication that the child's work needed correction. A few teachers, however, stressed to children that there was no 'right' or 'wrong' way and that all contributions from them were valuable. This was especially the case in mathematics or science investigation work.

Teachers told children that they were right, often by simply saying '*Right*', '*Yes*' or '*Spot on!*' or they might nod or smile instead. An evaluative phrase of praise, such as just saying, '*Good girl*' or sometimes, '*Thank you*', was a similar means. Teachers used this strategy through verbal, non-verbal and written means, and it was usually with individuals. In verbal situations, a common strategy was for the teacher to repeat the child's correct verbal response; some teachers consolidated this by then writing it on the blackboard or asking the child to do so. A few teachers fed back when a response was correct by asking a question, for example by asking a pupil to explain her response in more detail because it was exactly right. On written work, ticks were a common means of showing a child that his or her response was right. Some teachers gave ticks as the children were working in class.

The function of this strategy was to sort the correct from the incorrect. Teachers described to children that their response was right or good to confirm attainment of a desirable outcome. One Y2 teacher felt that this helped children '. . . to know what's acceptable and what would be a good idea to do'. The function of telling a child he or she was wrong was to pinpoint an area of weakness, following assessment, in order subsequently to enable improvement in the specific area of difficulty. Teachers could only feed back to children that they were right or wrong if they had already made some assessment. This assessment could be of the whole class or of an individual. Assessment strategies therefore preceded, and teaching strategies followed on from, the use of this feedback strategy.

A few Y6 teachers gave no comments on science work, only a tick at the end. This may have reflected the belief that there was no 'right' and 'wrong' in science investigations, and therefore the teacher accepted a wide range of responses as acceptable. In contrast, some teachers felt that right and wrong were clear in mathematics and therefore feedback could be more precise. Yet it was in mathematics that teachers told us they avoided putting crosses, putting only ticks so that they did not demotivate learning.

d) Describing why an answer is correct

The distinguishing feature of descriptive feedback in contrast to evaluative feedback, is that the feedback provides a description of why a particular judgement has been made. As mentioned above, teachers were aware of the different functions of evaluative and descriptive feedback and the need for both. When teachers described to children what was good about their achievements, their description was often accompanied by an evaluative phrase of praise. For example, a Y6 teacher said to one child, but in front of the whole class, 'Good girl! You've used 'freckly' and 'polished' which is a very good description of the top side of leaves'.

Teachers could use the strategy of describing why an answer is correct, verbally or in writing. The teacher could also describe why the work of the whole class was good, not just an individual within it. For example, at the end of a speaking and listening lesson based around antique objects, a Y6 teacher told the whole class, '*I was very pleased with the way you spoke out. It was like The Antiques Road Show*'.

With written work, teachers annotated work, rather than just giving a tick if it was right. With regard to written descriptions of why an answer was correct, we observed a comment for some creative writing, '*Well written, lots of detail and good vocabulary*' and for science, '*Good, you have carefully compared the two rocks*'. These were in contrast to evaluative comments which were not accompanied by description, such as simply, '*Well done*' or '*Good*'. One Y2 teacher wrote a list of 'Achievements' at the back of each child's exercise book in which she specified precisely where each individual child had done well.

Several teachers used one child's correct response to teach the class, by explaining to the whole class why the one child's response was good. For example, a Y6 teacher announced to the whole class that one boy had used the word 'decreased' instead of 'gone down', which was an achievement in his use of mathematical language. Teachers therefore used this feedback strategy in order to confirm a child's achievement, but also to inform children about acceptable performance. In this way, pupils learned what they should produce again, but also learned how to extend their achievement further. We observed teachers who habitually extended the good answers that pupils gave so as to contextualise them and show why they were appropriate, as well as to provide new and connected information. This was a common strategy at the beginning of a new lesson.

A few teachers directed children specifically to look at the comments they had made on their written work. They told us they believed that children were not only informed, but also motivated by receiving a personal written message that described their attainments, or by a written dialogue which encouraged discussion about their attainments.

Teachers used this strategy in several contexts, but it was particularly frequent in connection with one teaching strategy: when teachers asked children to read out or describe examples. They used this particularly when children were sitting together at the beginning or end of a lesson, but also as they circulated and looked at children's work. In each case, they described why one child's answer was good in order to confirm what was good about it and also to inform other children. Describing to the child why an answer was correct demanded that teachers had made quite a detailed assessment of the child's achievement first of all.

Understandably, it tended to be Y2 teachers who questioned the usefulness of written feedback comments on children's work. They suggested that either children could not read comments or that they did not bother. There were a couple of Y2 teachers, however, who felt that written comments were valuable, especially if they were then used as part of a dialogue. In general, though, Y2 teachers were more likely than Y6 teachers to write a feedback comment which acted as a note for themselves, while Y6 teachers were likely to write lengthier feedback comments to the pupils themselves. So both Y2 and Y6 teachers wrote feedback comments on children's work, though not on every piece of work.

e) Telling children what they have achieved and have not achieved

Teachers fed back to children by telling them what they had achieved or not achieved. They gave this type of feedback to individuals, pairs and groups or the whole class, and it could be verbal or written or both. By definition this feedback was of a descriptive nature. In using this strategy, teachers told children how far they had met pre-specified learning intentions or formal targets, worked within time targets or even achieved National Curriculum levels. Whether using 'learning intentions' or 'targets', teachers recognised that, in giving this kind of descriptive feedback, they told children that there were '. . . some things that you can be positive about and some things to work on in the future'.

Several teachers stressed the importance, therefore, of stating learning intentions in advance of a lesson, and specifically. At the end, they summed up what had, and also what had not, been learnt in a lesson, often in relation to learning intentions. One teacher described the summing up as the '. . . sharing of what we intended to do and what actually has happened'. A Y2 teacher told the whole class what their combined findings from a mathematics investigation had been, before praising everyone for a good morning's work. At the individual level, one Y6 teacher summarised for a child, 'Yes. You have found two words that mean "house"'. And a Y6 teacher presented a 'Got it!' stamp to anyone who seemed to have grasped a specified concept well.

Some teachers told children what they had or had not achieved in relation to targets. These were targets which had been achieved or targets which they set for the child, in order to clarify where the child needed to progress to next. These might be individual targets or more general ones. Teachers described clearly to the child what these targets represented, for example, if the target was National Curriculum Level 4 in writing, then the teacher described the criteria represented by Level 4 in writing. Time targets were another kind of target, that teachers fed back about how well children were achieving. They stressed to children what they should achieve within a set time limit.

The function of this strategy was to inform the child what he or she had learnt in relation to a specific goal, and what he or she still had not learnt in relation to a specific goal. The intended outcomes of using this strategy were:

- to celebrate a child's achievements;
- to motivate children by showing them how far they had already come;
- to clarify to children where they were aiming;
- to order targets in their heads; and
- to consolidate or reaffirm whatever had been learnt.

One Y6 teacher described how:

> It's helpful to them to give a brief summary, overview of what they have done, . . . 'Why have we been doing it? What have I learnt? Oh yes, that's what I learnt'. And by doing that, you are getting them to be able to recall it at another stage, it's easier for them to pick it up and recall it . . .

To use this strategy, teachers described needing initially to make a careful assessment in relation to learning intentions or targets. Once the gap between achievement and target had been identified, teachers were in a position to specify or imply a better way of doing things to children (or invite children to make suggestions); or to begin teaching a new topic. Because of its summarising function, this strategy was often used at the end of a session or day, or at the beginning of a consolidation lesson. It was the Y6 teachers who most often described the summarising function of this strategy and also the setting of time targets against which to measure children's achievements. The strategy was useful for all the core subjects, but writing and handwriting were mentioned most often in connection with this strategy.

f) Specifying or implying a better way of doing something

We observed teachers specifying or implying to children how they could improve a piece of work or a skill. They did this both verbally and in writing, addressing individuals usually, but also the whole group sometimes. By its nature, this type of feedback was descriptive. It was Y2 teachers who stressed the role of discussion as a vehicle for specifying or implying a better way of doing something, while it was the Y6 teachers who felt it was useful to write specific details in children's exercise books, about doing something a better way. Some teachers told us they wrote a note to their pupils, inviting them to 'see me', or come and discuss a better way of doing something with them.

We observed teachers advising children to begin a task again. For example, one Y2 teacher in a handwriting lesson wrote the first letter in a row of the same letter, where the child had written his own row incorrectly. Teachers redemonstrated or re-explained a task for the child to try anew, thus specifying a better way of doing the task.

Teachers also pointed out what was missing in children's work or skills, while recognising what was not missing first. They explained how a task might have been done better and they might advise the children to try a specific exercise or method or to practise a particular skill. For example, in a creative writing lesson, a Y6 teacher advised the class to concentrate on 'technical' skills. Another Y6 teacher suggested to a child that it would help him if he used pictures as cues when reading. Yet another Y6 teacher suggested to her pupil that she use a dictionary to help her spell.

In some cases, the teacher modelled a correct answer, demonstrated how to do a task (both 'teaching' strategies) or provided an alternative to show the child how to improve, sometimes asking the child to compare his or her own performance with the teacher's model. For example, she wrote out spellings or handwriting patterns for children to practise.

In other cases, the teacher drew on the child's own response, but then showed how it could be even better. For example, we observed one Y6 teacher who praised a pupil's piece of writing, then told her that she had used the same word six times and prompted her to think of other ways to replace the word. Sometimes the teacher implied a better way of doing something by refocusing a child onto the task they were supposed to be doing. Or she might adapt a child's response so that it better fulfilled a learning intention. For example, in a Y6 science investigation, the teacher suggested to one group of children that they continue with what they were doing, but just change one variable which would enhance 'the experiment.

The function of the strategy was to enable pupils to learn better and do better. Teachers specified or implied a better way of doing something by showing pupils:

- how to make specific corrections;
- how to meet a newly set target;
- or how to move forward towards a more extended achievement.

Some teachers suggested that by writing targets for individual children, constructive criticism could be positive. For example, by writing out the words which a child needed to study because he or she got them wrong, the child could see correction of errors more as a challenge than as a criticism.

Teachers seemed to use this feedback strategy for all subjects. They tended to use it mostly at the beginning of a lesson or of teaching a subject, or during the process, so that children could act immediately on their specifications or implications for a better way of doing things. This was because this strategy had to follow an assessment of a child's achievements.

Some teaching strategies were also implicated in using this strategy: specifying or implying a better way of doing something does involve the teacher in using the teaching strategies of modelling, remodelling, directing children to further practising and relaying ways of learning. This feedback strategy's prime function is, however, imparting a judgement about how a specific achievement could be improved. In some cases, it could lead to children then suggesting their own ways for improvement.

g) Getting children to suggest ways they can improve

Teachers who used this strategy asked individuals to feed back to them about ways they could improve. Teachers sometimes asked a group or the whole class. For example, a Y6 teacher challenged the whole class to think of strategies to help them remember to put capitals and full stops in their creative writing; and then asked each individual to name what it was they needed to improve on, in addition to remembering capitals and full stops. Usually, however, teachers used this strategy on an individual basis, either verbally or in written form.

In order to get children to suggest (or describe) ways in which they could improve, teachers used:

- commands, such as 'Go back and check your work';
- invitations, such as 'Tell me how . . .', or
- questions, such as 'What would make this better?'

Sometimes teachers asked children to relate suggested improvement to a target and some invited children to set their own targets. We observed one Y2 teacher who did this on a regular basis (although on occasions she made suggestions for the child), by writing the proposed targets at the front of each child's mathematics and English exercise books. For other teachers, it was less formalised. A Y6 teacher explained,

> I may talk to them individually and say to them, 'What do you want to do next?' or 'How could you now go and improve this work?' I probably wouldn't actually call it a target.

In these ways, teachers asked children to say what was right or wrong in their work, why their work was correct or incorrect, how it could be better, or to describe the next steps towards achieving a target not yet met. This type of feedback was therefore necessarily descriptive.

The function of the strategy was to encourage self-evaluation in that the child became self-critical and thus self-directed in their learning. A Y6 teacher explained,

> . . . sometimes I ask them to go back and look at what they did wrong and see if they can correct it and I always say, 'Do you know why you made that mistake?'.

Asking children a question whereby they discuss with the teacher, for example, why they made a mistake, was one means of getting children to discuss how they could improve. Teachers tried to get children to discuss ways they could improve so that their thinking was challenged. A Y2 teacher explained she would be

> . . . talking to them about what they had done and, by questioning processes, I'd be able to move them on and ask, 'So what if . . . ?' or 'How could you move this on?' or 'How could you change that in order to make it better?'.

We observed the following written comment with the same function, *'A good attempt, but there are still some improvements that can be made. Any ideas?'*. This, however, would need to lead to a discussion with the child.

Some teachers provided a model for a child and asked the child to talk about the difference between the model and their own work: for example, one Y6 teacher listened to a child read her poem, then read it out himself, and asked her, *'How do you think you could have read that better?'*.

On the whole, teachers used this strategy in the middle of the lesson, especially through questioning, as part of the teaching and feedback that was integral to the lesson. Teachers seemed to get children to suggest ways in which they could improve more during lessons where they were consolidating knowledge than during lessons where new knowledge was being presented. This was because teachers could not expect 'improvement' if a basic level of competence had not already been reached.

This strategy could also be categorised as a teaching strategy, in that the teacher was 'getting children to do' something. It does not, however, fit with our definition of a teaching strategy as 'a presentation, in various ways, of adult-decided knowledge, skills and understanding'. However, the teacher was getting children to 'impart directly a judgement of the child's strategies, skills or attainment and give information about that judgement'. That is, children were receiving feedback, only in this case it was through the prompting of the teacher. The judgement by the child nearly always followed an assessment made by the teacher (or the child).

Teachers used this strategy in the context of writing in particular, although they used it in other subject areas too. Perhaps surprisingly, almost equal numbers of teachers from each year group described getting children to be self-critical about their work and used discussion to provoke children's thoughts about how they could improve.

CONCLUSION

To summarise, we described two feedback strategies of an evaluative type. This meant that in using them, teachers helped children to feel either good or bad, but did not refer to the work itself. These strategies were:

- giving rewards and punishments,
- expressing approval and disapproval.

Teachers used these strategies primarily:

- to motivate children and boost their self-esteem as people and learners, when they gave rewards and expressed approval; or

- to discourage them from showing learning behaviour which was not acceptable to the teacher, when they gave punishments and expressed disapproval.

There were also five feedback strategies whose function was descriptive. That is, in using these strategies, teachers were giving children more or less information about the standard of their achievements (in relation to more or less specific criteria and looking towards improvement). These strategies were:

- telling children they are right or wrong;
- describing why an answer is correct;
- telling children what they have or have not achieved;
- specifying or implying a better way of doing something; and
- getting children to suggest ways they can improve.

By telling children they were right or wrong, teachers sorted the correct from the incorrect, so that children knew which paths to follow in future and which they would need to think about again. Teachers then described to children why their answers were correct in order to confirm the child's achievement, but also to inform the child about what an acceptable performance consisted of. Teachers told children what they had or had not achieved, in order to inform them what they had learnt in relation to a specific goal, and what they still had not learnt in relation to a specific goal. In relation to the areas where children had not yet achieved, the teacher could now feed back by specifying or implying a better way of doing something and then get the children to suggest ways themselves in which they could improve.

This conceptual progression from giving personal, evaluative comments for motivational or control purposes, to inviting children to suggest how they could improve their own work with reference to specific targets, reflects the range of feedback types represented on Tunstall and Gipps' typology of feedback (see Table 5.1). It is important to note, however, that the typology deals with feedback *types*, while this chapter deals with feedback *strategies*. The typology describes actions and

Table 5.1 A typology of assessment feedback (Tunstall and Gipps, 1996) adapted to show the relationship between feedback types and feedback strategies

Type	Evaluative Feedback				Descriptive Feedback			
	A1	A2	B1	B2	C1	C2	D1	D2
	Rewarding (positive)	Punishing (negative)	Approving (positive)	Disapproving (negative)	Specifying attainment	Specifying improvement	Mutual construction of achievement	Mutual construction of improvement
Dedicated feedback strategies	Giving rewards	Giving punishments	Expressing approval	Expressing disapproval	Telling children they are right/ wrong; Describing why an answer is correct; Telling children what they have/have not achieved	Specifying or implying a better way of doing something	[e.g. Discussing with children the features of a piece of work]	Getting children to suggest ways they can improve

aspects which help define feedback types, while this chapter describes strategies that teachers actually use to give the feedback itself.

Table 5.1 shows how the feedback strategies described in this chapter fit into the spectrum of feedback types represented in the typology. The types of feedback shown, and the corresponding strategies, shift towards the increasingly proactive participation of the pupil, and the increasingly supportive rather than directive role of the teacher. Although in practice, teachers used a range of feedback strategies in each lesson, conceptually we perceive this progression from strategies dominated by the teacher's authority over a 'passive' pupil to those which rely on the pupil's engagement and initiation.

With all evaluative feedback, rewarding, punishing, approving and disapproving, the teacher is feeding back her own, personal judgement about work.

With descriptive feedback where the teacher is specifying attainment or improvement, the teacher is *telling children [something]*, *describing* and *specifying*, and may refer the child to an outside authority, such as a learning target. Then the child may evaluate the feedback in relation to the target and recognise the gap between what is achieved and what is not yet achieved. This feedback type is one in which the teacher tells (and the pupil receives).

With descriptive feedback where the teacher and pupil are discussing or 'constructing' attainment or improvement *mutually*, the child's role is integral to the feeding back process itself. The child is being encouraged and supported in making a self-assessment or self-evaluation by reflecting on his or her performance in relation to the standard expected (and indicated by the teacher), and thinking about how performance can improve. This end of the feedback spectrum therefore involves children in using *metacognitive* strategies, whereby they monitor or regulate their own learning. They are now *supported* by the teacher but not *dependent* on her, in deciding on the value of a performance and how it could improve.

In the next chapter, we unpack teachers' and pupils' views about how children learn best. We consider the importance of this development, where children take initiative in, and responsibility for, their own learning and how teachers believe they can encourage children along this path.

Chapter 6

Learning and teaching: Teachers' and pupils' views

INTRODUCTION

As well as finding out how these teachers organised their lessons and did their teaching we wanted to know whether this linked in with views about learning. How did these teachers think children learned? Did the teaching strategies they used coincide with theories of learning, or indeed 'common sense' views of learning? And also, what did the children have to say about how they learned?

We found that the teachers very rarely named learning theories or theorists even when invited to. Our data suggests that the teachers were not conversant with formal theories of learning 'chapter and verse', and that, although half said they found theories of learning useful, the majority did not allow particular learning theories to guide their practice directly. However, the detailed analysis of the interviews and other research data allowed close scrutiny of their beliefs about learning styles, motivation, social interaction, and children's thinking. This indicated that teachers use learning theory intuitively; at some time all of them were working, if unconsciously, with elements of formal theory.

TEACHERS' VIEWS

Teachers' beliefs about learning can be summarised as: **Children learn in a range of ways,** and so **learning requires a combination of different teaching strategies.** Teachers' views were that children learn: **When the teacher relays information; when the teacher intervenes constantly; when the teacher gives them feedback.** The teachers also talked about children's learning strategies. Children learn:

- through play;
- by listening;
- through interaction;
- by doing;
- by practising;
- by copying adults and others;
- through being critical of their own work;
- when they initiate their own learning;
- by thinking;
- by building up knowledge step-by-step;
- by making connections.

They also talked about conditions for learning. Children learn when:

- they feel motivated,
- they feel safe to take risks.

Children learn in different ways

The key underlying view was: 'Children learn differently from each other. Full stop!'.

This was a belief held by all of our teachers. The general feeling was that in any classroom there is inevitably a range of learning styles. Teachers described children who learned better by passively listening to the teacher and other children who learned easily by absorbing information from a group: 'the classic case of the "penny dropping" during interaction and listening to others'. They named children who could cogitate and ponder over a problem and see their way to a solution, other children who, faced with the same problem, would want to 'draw a little picture' and had a visual learning style, and still others who would want to verbalise their ideas and rehearse them aloud. They described lateral thinkers and children who learned by building knowledge step by step. They knew children who were help-seekers and benefited from a great deal of teacher explanation and clarification and children who 'wouldn't ask' but needed one-to-one input and constant intervention. They explained that different learners seemed to require different types of teacher feedback: some thrived in a competitive atmosphere where there was the possibility of rewards for good work, others needed constant praise and 'nothing negative at all'.

This differentiation went as far as teachers reporting that different children had different ways of learning the same subject. In relation to spelling, a Y6 teacher concluded that some children learned by being taught how to spell and given repeated encouragement to 'physically look' at words, while others had some kind of innate aptitude for it, suggesting that some children had a better memory for word patterns than others and perhaps used visual clues more successfully.

With reading, a Y2 teacher explained: 'I think children learn to read in different ways . . . grabbing on to different strategies' and another infant teacher gave an illustration of the different strategies used by two boys:

> I've got a child at the moment who reads purely by sound and he doesn't look at the pattern of the whole word . . . and then another – he can only learn from sight vocabulary. He has about 60 words that he recognises by sight and although he just about knows his sounds, he is not able to use those sounds at all.

A third Y2 teacher theorised that children who had learned to read became different kinds of learners from children who hadn't; the ability to read was a catalyst to other learning. As she put it,

> Children think differently when they have learned to read. Something happens inside the brain and they actually function in a different way – they can reason, they can understand abstract ideas so much more easily.

Two Y6 teachers specifically raised an issue about 'Using and Applying Maths' (AT1). Their point was that some learners find this easy and others do not, so their learning strategies must be different. Both teachers tussled with the idea. One found it too difficult to think through but the other hypothesised that children who find maths problems easy imagine the problem as a real life situation and can make a connection between the problem and the numerical process required, whereas children who did not sense 'a natural connection' were the ones who found applying maths difficult.

Furthermore when teachers considered one individual child's learning across subjects, they could see that she or he was better at some things than others. For example, they cited children who learned about shape and measures easily but found number work more difficult, children who could read well but found some maths topics very hard and children who were very good at practical science but who found recording their findings difficult. Teachers theorised that these individual learners must be using different strategies in different subjects, some appropriate and some which did not work. The task of the teacher was to delve, probe and find out about the child's learning strategies in order to introduce new and more appropriate methods to help the child. One way of doing this was to mix different learners in the same group, with a view to learners learning from each other's different methods. This was often the case for science when children had different levels of skill – some were better at observation, some at hypothesising, some at predicting. In this context, teachers believed that children learned from listening and discussing.

In summary, all the teachers had strong beliefs that the children in their class were different types of learner using different learning strategies, echoing Gardner's theory of multiple intelligences. Moreover teachers reasoned that each individual child used different strategies sometimes appropriately and sometimes inappropriately, particularly in relation to different subjects.

We asked the teachers whether boys learned in a different way from girls. Teachers found this quite a difficult topic. However, three teachers (two Y2 and one Y6) stated clearly that, although they were aware of stereotyping, they believed that boys **did** learn differently from girls, and this was biological, it was 'something in their genes' or 'something in their make up'. One of the Y2 teachers explained:

> I suppose a lot of it is to do with stereotyping, but I also do believe that physiologically, intellectually . . . they are actually different . . . they do actually function in a different way.

Over half the teachers (from both year groups) were of the opinion that 'ways of learning are not down to gender' – children of both sexes are individual learners and use different approaches and different learning strategies; it was simply up to the teacher to discern and cater for the learning styles of individuals. Both boys and girls could be very visual, both girls and boys could learn through hands-on experience, both boys and girls could 'work things out' for themselves. The teachers could see no genetic reason why girls should learn differently from boys. They also thought that girls and boys had learned to act differently because of cultural stereotyping and this led teachers to expect certain behaviour of them, but it was not necessarily learning behaviour. The teachers stressed that it was important for them to be aware of these stereotypes and avoid allowing them to influence their teaching. A Y2 teacher reported:

If we go in expecting boys to learn differently and expecting them to be more boisterous, then they live up to those expectations. I have some equally challenging boys and girls and they all seem to be progressing.

A quarter of the teachers also reported that boys '*dominated*' sessions when teachers asked for contributions, boys '*hogged the computer*' or boys were 'boisterous' in class. Girls were noticeably '*more passive*', quiet and studious. These (female) teachers felt it was their duty to compensate and so intervened, for example, making sure that they questioned girls by name to ensure a contribution, organising turn taking on the computers and setting girls construction tasks. Their treatment of boys and girls was different in other ways, for example one teacher never allowed boys to choose partners, others were aware that they gave boys more attention.

In summary, teachers were quite widely divided over the differences between boys and girls as learners: only a minority believed that learning style was related to gender. Other teachers, preferring to see each child as an individual and idiosyncratic learner, tried to counteract stereotypical notions of boys and girls in the ways that they viewed learners. Others, accepting the stereotypes, gave boys and girls different treatment.

During the discussion, several teachers reported being confused by research. A Y6 teacher had read that boys might be using '*a different side of the brain*' from girls and was not sure how this entered the conundrum. Many teachers were aware that girls achieve better than boys in national assessment and examinations and this had made them wonder if boys' and girls' learning strategies *could* somehow be different, although their own experience of teaching at primary level had not supported this.

Because of their views about individuals learning in different ways, teachers talked about the different teaching strategies needed.

Learning requires a combination of different teaching strategies

Most Y2 and Y6 teachers said they believed that children learned when teachers applied a *combination* of different teaching methods, approaches, styles, techniques, or broad strategies. Teachers expressed this belief in various terms. One Y6 teacher believed that '. . . *you have to try a whole variety of things and variety itself is one of the things that you have to try*'. Another considered teaching to be '. . . *an exceptionally complex range of activities which requires the ability to have many strategies, approaches, in place all the time'.* One Y6 teacher explained, 'You've got to say, "How can I approach that idea again in a different way, or how could I structure that lesson in a different way?".'

Y2 and Y6 teachers believed that using a combination of different teaching strategies helped children learn in that it entailed finding approaches that were suitable or that *'worked'* for the particular learning of the individual or class. This enabled teachers to discard inappropriate styles. One Y2 teacher said,

> I think I may have a way that I think works but I will always find a child that it doesn't work with, so I have to go back to the drawing board and think again.

Teachers also had the theory that if a lesson were presented using a variety of methods or techniques, the point of the lesson was more likely to be drummed home. One Y2 teacher expressed it as follows:

> . . . you've just got to be prepared to find as many different ways as you can of presenting the same material in the hope that they will see it from another angle.

At least five teachers commented that, sometimes, peers could provide another angle which the teacher as an adult could not. They also suggested that by teaching the same mathematics lesson using different apparatus, the point would be more likely to be made than by using only one type.

Finally, a few teachers saw variety of methods or styles as essential to children's motivation in learning:

> It is the very changing of it, the keeping it interesting, that can be one of the things that can help you convey the knowledge or can help you invite children to learn.

(Y6 teacher)

Children learn when the teacher relays information

Three-quarters of our teachers believed that, in some circumstances at least, children learn when the teacher 'relays information' as in traditional teaching. They had a variety of theories as to which purposes this strategy served best and believed that mathematics was the subject it served best.

A Y6 teacher told us that,

> . . . there are occasions where we get our learning through 'sitting at the feet of the master' and hearing things that we might take ages to work out for ourselves, being explained by somebody who can explain well. So there are those occasions, but there are lots of other ways that children learn, too, and it is important that that isn't seen as the only way.

Other teachers echoed this sentiment: several teachers said that relaying information needed to be followed by allowing the child to work alone. Another set of teachers felt that relaying information should be accompanied by the children finding out for themselves in discovery learning. Others again suggested that it should be balanced by sessions of discussion and interaction among pupils and between teacher and pupils.

There were three main purposes for which teachers chose to use the strategy of relaying information. First, to introduce a new lesson. One teacher explained why she had relayed information about tens and units:

> That then was just sort of an introduction to the lesson. So it was almost to get their minds into thinking of tens and units and how numbers are made up so that when they go to their activity, they are focused on thinking about tens and units.

Second, to relay information about how pupils should go about doing a task and what they should avoid.

> I think they do need teacher input, a lot of work on how they can improve strategies that they use and it really does need to be this 'listening to the teacher . . .

Third, when a pupil, or even the whole class, had run into difficulties. If they could not learn independently, then the strategy of relaying information could be used as a remedy.

But the most common view was that relaying information was particularly useful for the learning of mathematics. Although a few teachers mentioned times when the strategy benefited the learning of spelling, handwriting, reading, writing, science and even speaking and listening, mathematics was the subject which most teachers agreed benefited from this approach. A Y6 teacher described how:

I often do this in maths, if I find something that is not known or has been lost somewhere and not been covered, then I bring the whole class together and almost in the formal situation, [I say]: 'Look, we've got to get to grips with this . . .'

Children learn when the teacher intervenes constantly

At least two-thirds of the teachers in our sample told us they believed that, in some circumstances at least, children learned when the teacher intervened constantly.

The most commonly described type of intervention was that of teachers circulating around the class, supervising or monitoring what individual children were doing. When they saw a need to intervene, they would give direction or guidance, show a child an example, discuss a topic with a child, ask the child questions, give stimulation or give direct input.

A couple of teachers felt that intervention was necessary to make sure children covered enough work,

I think you need to be focusing them all the time, walking round the classroom, keeping them on the task in hand, keeping them talking about what they are supposed to be talking about.

(Y6)

One remarked that this was especially necessary with boys who were 'lazier' than girls.

In some situations, intervention was only necessary if a child was going wrong.

. . . like number formation . . . if I see it going wrong, then I usually pick up on it as and when I see it, because the more they do it incorrectly then it is just reinforced for them.

(Y2)

In other cases, the teacher believed she needed to intervene to help poorer learners keep up with the rest of their group. Where intervention was seen as correction or remedial teaching, teachers were implying that the majority of children were getting on well with their work. Teachers also recognised, though, that even children who could work well independently needed to be moved forward beyond what they could do alone, through the teacher's intervention.

Children will learn by discovering things for themselves in the sense that dry sand will pour and wet sand won't pour. That's probably all they'll discover about sand and then, in order to move that learning forward, you need to have some intervention. There needs to be some challenge . . . They need intervention to move on from that basic understanding.

(Y2)

Several teachers believed that intervention was useful for learning in the form of constant reminders to the whole class about important points:

. . . children can't concentrate, they can't retain all the advice, so it is quite useful, I feel, to punctuate the lessons by reminding them how they annotate and it doesn't matter how many times you do this. I think at their age they do forget and they need advice.

(Y6)

A quarter of the teachers, mainly Y6, believed however, that children could learn without the intervention of the teacher, if the learning task was well planned and did not require, for example, the teacher's practical guidance. One Y2 teacher stressed that children could learn without the teacher's intervention if the task they were working on was neither too easy nor too hard. The same Y2 teacher went on to comment that when children worked without her intervention,

I think they probably develop confidence-wise, they need time to consolidate and I think that is part of intellectual development.

In other words, the process of working independently 'without constant intervention', was a part of learning. Another teacher agreed that

. . . you must not think that you need to hear everything they say because that is part of their development, to work without adult input all the time.

Children learn when the teacher gives them feedback

All the teachers believed that feedback was important to children's learning. Teachers had various theories, however, about how feedback should be given, when it should be given and what its specific purposes were, if children were to learn as a result.

Teachers agreed that feedback which encouraged was essential, while realistic or honest feedback was more useful than constant praise, in the view of both Y2 and Y6 teachers. . . .

> children learn by realistic acceptance of where they are and where they used to be and how to move on and for different children that will be different.
>
> (Y6)

Critical feedback was also helpful, and in some cases even negative feedback.

> . . . negative feedback will result in positive reaction. It doesn't always, but my experience is that most often negative is as important as positive.
>
> (Y2)

At least 10 teachers, mostly Y6 teachers, felt that children learned when the teacher gave feedback through the medium of other children. The teacher might invite children to comment on each others' work; she might draw an individual's attention to a feedback comment she had made to the whole class; or most commonly, she might show an individual's work as an example for the whole class, which they could use as a guide as to what was acceptable or good. One Y6 teacher suggested not only using models of children's good work, but '. . . the class together can suggest ways that the person can improve their learning' or they might learn by hearing about an individual's problem. Feedback could also be in the form of the teacher weaving children's contributions into her delivery, for example, by linking children's comments to pieces of learning that the teacher considered important or basing a piece of work on one child's good idea.

> You must take the [child's] contribution and act on it if you can. Children's contributions help the others to learn.
>
> (Y6)

Both groups of teachers described written feedback as helping children to learn, but understandably the teachers of younger children were more likely to express the need to read over written comments with the child if it was to be really useful. They also emphasised, more than teachers of older children, the benefits of immediate, verbal feedback.

Many teachers believed that a dedicated feedback plenary at the end of a lesson or session was beneficial for learning. The advantages came about by

> . . . bringing children together at the end of a session, feeding back, showing the other children what's going on, what other children have done and using their work to help the rest of the children, positively and praising.
>
> (Y2)

> . . . if they are not given time to stop and think and reflect and to see others work as well as themselves, and see examples of what good work is, or what I perceive good work to be, then they are a bit lost really.
>
> (Y2)

The plenary feedback session was to consolidate children's earlier learning. Through the teacher's feedback, or the feedback she invited other children to give, the session could remind the class '. . . *of the concept that they should have learnt at the beginning of the lesson*' (Y6); or it could remind the children of what they had actually learnt; or '. . . *just in case there was somebody hanging onto the net, you could pull them up*' (Y6).

Feedback as an aid to learning

Teachers felt that feedback aided learning in four ways:

- **by encouraging and motivating children through praise so that they have self-esteem and the confidence to learn;**

> Depending on the child, some children need constant praise and nothing negative at all, whereas somebody else can cope with a bit of both. But all children need positive feedback, to sort of inspire them, on a regular basis.
>
> (Y6)

> If you've got a child who is struggling . . . then that child needs to know that you have spotted that they are having difficulty.
>
> (Y2)

- **by highlighting children's mistakes so that they can improve on weak areas of learning;**

*If you constantly give praise and encouragement, are they actually
learning anything unless you specify what's wrong?*

(Y6)

In this the teacher was referring to 'descriptive' feedback in which the
child receives information about how to move from actual achievement
to expected achievement. Other teachers referred to the need for being
specific about the kind of improvement they were looking for, as outlined in the previous chapter.

Several teachers believed that pupils should also be directed to
detect their own mistakes. Teachers usually expressed the belief that
criticism should be given together with praise.

> *. . . it needs her to see how those corrections are made and for me to
> say, 'Have a look back and see where you went wrong'. But also for
> her to know that I am really very pleased with it overall. If you tackle
> it this way, you still preserve motivation.*

(Y2)

- **by moving children on to the next stage of a learning experience,
  perhaps with reference to their progress;**

Y2 teachers described feeding back to children how much progress they
had made, especially in relation to handwriting, perhaps showing pupils
the work they had produced earlier in the term or year and comparing
it with current work. Many teachers believed that feedback was important in the whole process of moving children forward, by helping them
to see the next step clearly.

> *. . . if you didn't understand it and there's been no assistance in moving
> towards understanding, it's not very likely that you are going to under-
> stand it now . . . that's a sort of feedback element.*

(Y6)

- **by providing children with a clear idea of what is expected of
  them and what they have achieved;**

Connected to the belief about feedback helping to move children forward, was the belief that feedback could help children learn by showing them what was expected of them, or laying out clear targets for
them.

. . . feedback is helpful to the child [since] the child knows where he or she stands and what perhaps I want next from them, what I expect from them.
(Y2)

This belief was held by Y2 and Y6 teachers equally. Two teachers actually used individually-tailored, and accessible targets which they wrote on children's work so that children could refer to them and aim towards them. Two other teachers described how negative feedback could demonstrate what was not acceptable, both to the child who produced it and to others who saw the teacher's response.

Children's learning strategies: the teachers' view

Over the course of the research it became clear that all 24 teachers held the belief that children can take in new knowledge and develop skills and understanding in many different ways. To quote one Y6 teacher: *'There are many ways of being a learner'*. Teachers described solo learning strategies (such as listening, doing, practising, copying another person), unconscious learning strategies (such as thinking, building up knowledge step by step, making connections between bits of knowledge), and interactive strategies (such as listening and discussing in a group or in play situations).

It was generally felt that the challenge for the teacher was to provide opportunities for different ways of learning. This theory clearly underpinned the lessons we observed when teachers varied the learning opportunities to include, among other things, *'the one where you are a little passive and you are just able to sit quietly and listen and the [other] sort of interactive thing'*. We observed opportunities for children to interact, discuss and listen to each other both during brainstorming activities in all core subjects and while carrying out experiments and investigations in maths and science; we observed opportunities for children to answer questions and give contributions in whole-class teaching situations (all core subjects); and we observed opportunities for children to think and turn things over in their minds during solo problem solving and writing tasks. At times, the ways in which the teachers grouped the pupils seemed to fit the type of learning opportunity (group work for listening and discussing; whole-class teaching for passive listening; individual work for thinking and problem solving) but it was not always clear whether this was intentional, whether it was routine or for reasons of curriculum management. We could not always tell if children were learning, but, when interviewed, children of both age groups explained that they could learn in these different ways and contexts.

a) Children learn through play

A few of the teachers of younger children expressed the view that young children learn through play, seeing playing as a first step to learning a skill, as with writing. '*I think children learn to write through practice "play" writing . . . and this is really beneficial, just having a go and not being judged on what they have done'.*

In another sense, play, '*structured*' to support the curriculum (classroom shops to play at '*spending*' money, sand play, water play, dressing up and so on) was seen as an important and vital process in infant learning. However, what is interesting (and unexpected), was how little the infant teachers talked about play, given popular stereotypes about the role of play in infant teaching and learning, and indeed the children themselves did not mention it.

b) Children learn by listening

There was no doubt in teachers' minds that children learn through listening. All teachers believed children could assimilate information by heeding and noting what people said. At times teachers of both age groups expected children to listen passively, to offer no contribution but to turn things over in their minds. As one explained:

> *In lessons where it starts with me out front, they know this is the bit where they must be really listening and they must be taking on the things that are said. I might say something like 'I'm going to suggest to you a way of doing this task . . . and I suggest you listen carefully and think about using this technique'.*

> (Y6)

c) Children learn through interacting

All the teachers were of the opinion that children also learn through interaction, by listening AND discussing with others; and that this interaction was a crucial part of learning. Teachers believed that listening enhanced learning because it allowed children to reflect and perhaps change their own opinions of things, while discussion/dialogue enhanced learning because it offered the chance to confer and perhaps argue a point and so promote thinking. In the words of a Y2 teacher: '*Listening, I think, is crucial to their learning because listening intensely promotes deeper thought; discussing clarifies the thought and possibly develops the thought*'. Some teachers theorised that the very act of verbalising ideas assisted learning. As teachers expressed it: '*If they say it to themselves, then it makes them think*' and '*They will deepen their ideas by expressing them*'. Because of this belief, one or two teachers reported that they would direct children to explain things to other children.

The whole notion of interaction was important in teachers' theories about learning because they believed that it led to children exchanging knowledge and sharing understandings, to listening, taking note, realising and achieving more. When explaining the value of paired work, a teacher explained: '*They bounce ideas off each other which helps them to develop intellectually*'. Teachers reported that, at times, they left children to work together in pairs or groups '*to question and talk about things*' without constantly intervening themselves. However at other times, teachers became players in the interaction, for example when they chaired whole class seminar-type discussions involving open-ended questioning or when they talked individually with a child. In this latter respect, teachers might bolster, validate or help a child to develop a '*discovery*' the child had made by talking it over with them. Equally, as part of teacher feedback, they might discuss and resolve problems a child was encountering – '*talk through their thinking with them*'.

In interview, teachers frequently illustrated their theories about learning through interaction by referring to different subjects. For example it was suggested that, in maths, children's understanding is improved both when they propose and articulate ways of solving problems and when they verbalise the processes they have been using to get to answers; it helps the speaker's thinking and it helps the listener's thinking. In maths and science investigations teachers believed that children learned through discussing and devising systems together, coming up with problems that they would encounter and rejecting some ideas because of problems connected with them. One or two teachers theorised that engagement with maths and science equipment in itself triggered thinking in group members, especially if children thought '*out loud*' and as they worked with the apparatus.

It was suggested by a few Y2 teachers that group reading could have an '*amazing*' effect on children as readers. Group reading involved listening, discussing and other forms of interaction. Children listened to other children reading a text they could themselves see; the teacher and children discussed many things such as meanings of words, phonic build-up of words, inference of parts of the text; interaction took the form of the teacher or other children giving explicit help by saying a word for someone stuck or by pointing at pictures, hinting that pictures can be used as cues. Overall, teachers felt that 'sharing books, talking about books is all a prompt to reading'.

One or two Year 6 teachers explained the importance of brainstorming before children embarked upon writing. They believed that imagination was *fed* by this kind of interaction. Brainstorming throwing out all your ideas on a topic in itself was a useful learning process, while listening to other people's ideas improved understanding and gave a different slant on the topic. The teachers believed that children learned how to improve their writing by sharing ideas with others. On occasion teachers suggested that children could learn from peer feedback. For example, when pairs were asked to check each other's writing, children were listening and discussing ways of improving their work.

d) Children learn by 'doing'

A widely prevailing view among the teachers and the children was that children learn through direct, hands-on experience and practical activities. Teachers believed in children '*doing experiments, trying things out, touching, feeling*', learning through the senses and generally coming to understand through doing. It was felt that 'doing' things made learning 'real'. '*I think that learning ought to be rooted in experience . . . when you have done something, you have then got much more of a handle on it*'. Teachers argued that children 'made sense' through engagement with different apparatus, materials and visual stimuli of all kinds – '*learning by doing, by really just doing and finding out, using every available resource there is; using the computer, using objects . . .*'. Teachers shared the view that experimentation led the learner to '*turn the ideas in their own heads*' and so hit upon truths; it was important '*for [children] to do it themselves and see it*'.

Beyond the widespread idea that children learn through 'doing', it was strongly argued by almost half the teachers that children learned 'more', 'better' or 'quicker' through practical encounters with maths and science activities than through passively listening to a teacher transmitting facts. '*They need to know how to measure something, how to do a fair test, not just in their heads but by doing*', explained a Y6 teacher, while a Y2 argued: '*for them to just sit and for me to tell them what I know, they won't learn as effectively as if I can involve them with handling things and doing*'. Teachers also suggested that children were more likely to remember and retain what they had learned by getting involved, handling things, 'getting their hands dirty' than by sitting listening to relayed information.

Learning by doing was particularly important for maths and science, *'they will learn a concept most effectively by doing an experiment, an investigation, making a model. All the knowledge acquisition is through doing it and having explosions on the table or whatever'*. In contrast to this last remark, another Y6 teacher was of the view that not all scientific knowledge could be learned through experimentation. She was the only teacher to raise this point and she explained:

> . . . *where you are handling things like batteries and circuits you can see what happens and this can be learned relatively easily, but things like forces are much more abstract. I really think children have a lot of difficulty with this, and how they learn it is often a little bit rote.*

Younger children might need more experience of manipulating apparatus than older children (who are likely to be more capable of abstract thinking). If, after an assessment, children of any age appeared to be having difficulties conceptualising mathematical ideas, teachers of both age groups felt it was a useful learning experience for them to *return* to manipulating concrete apparatus.

Teachers of both ages were agreed that through 'doing' and experimentation, children can discover things and find things out. However, teachers of older children were slightly more concerned to direct children's discoveries towards specified outcomes.

The idea that children could find things out or discover for themselves through experimentation was popular with all the teachers, but the role of the teacher in 'discovery learning' was seen slightly differently by different teachers, particularly in relation to the degree of guidance children should have. Half stressed that the classroom cannot be set up as a 'free for all' and that children cannot just be left alone to discover things; they might not discover what the teacher wanted them to. It was important to these teachers that they guided children towards the desired discovery. Seven other teachers believed, not in direction, but in questioning children as they were experimenting in an open way, making children think and theorise. In this case there was no desired discovery, rather the aim was for children to develop the techniques of inquiry. The remaining teachers saw their role as standing back and observing children before deciding on any contribution they might make. These teachers (of the younger children) believed in allowing children time to work through things, to get things wrong, to go back and change things.

e) Children learn through practising

A quarter of our teachers suggested that children learn through practising and revision, for example by repeating work on the same topic, by working through exercises and by returning to and 'going over' previous knowledge and understandings. Practice activities were given so that the child could: build up understanding or consolidate something already encountered ('Ah yes! I did this before, I can do it again and I _can do this_') or have further opportunity to grasp something not fully understood. As one teacher explained: '_They are learning through practice and then they get to a point when they say "Oh I know how to do it now"._'

Half the teachers specifically mentioned that children learned to read by practising, especially practising with another reader present who could aid the learning process. In the words of one Y6 teacher: '_Reading is [learned] through practice and time and one-to-one and sharing and listening_'. Because of their beliefs in practising many of the teachers had set up regular times for children to practise reading to a listener (another child, the teacher, a parent). At least three Y6 teachers had set up a silent reading session for fluent readers for a certain period of time every day, believing that practising is still a necessary learning strategy even if the basic skill of decoding has been mastered. Handwriting and spelling could also be improved by practice. A Y2 teacher believed that looking at and writing the same word over and over again helped children to learn to spell.

> I pick out three of the key spelling words they have been given and I leave missing gaps in them so they have got to keep writing the word again and again and again. I will put the word 'they' and I will put [for example] 'th –y' – so they have got to keep up with all the different combinations.

Maths was also something that could be learned by practising; children could learn how to carry out number operations by doing lots of them and it was felt that younger children could learn to write their numbers the right way round by practising from a model. One Y6 teacher stressed that by constantly reciting multiplication tables aloud, children could commit them to memory.

Y2 teachers were slightly more inclined towards practising as a key strategy in learning and this was probably because of their responsibility for children's consolidation of the basic skills, particularly reading. Y6 teachers were more likely to see practising as a useful learning strategy for children who had not learned things the first time (apart from the case of reading).

f) Children learn through copying others

Teachers believe children learned through copying other people: either the teacher, other adults or other children. When children were learning by copying the teacher, this tended to be in a whole-class setting. When they were learning by copying other pupils like themselves, this was usually in paired or group work. When they were copying from other pupils who were more able than themselves, this could be in a whole class, group or paired setting. Learning through copying from the teacher, other adults and more able children was mentioned by Y2 and Y6 teachers alike, but learning through copying from pupils of similar ability was more often mentioned by teachers of older children.

The subject context was nearly always language. Learning through copying occurred particularly when children were learning reading, speaking and writing, including creative writing especially, but also handwriting and spelling.

Modelling stories for pupils helped them both with their reading skills and their story writing skills.

> . . . really it is just modelling reading and getting them to enjoy it, getting them to predict using the picture cues and perhaps initial letters, although quite a few of the group are not sure of the initial letters. Just beginning to demonstrate early reading strategies for them and hoping that they are having an enjoyable experience, perhaps picking up a few of those strategies along the way.
>
> (Y2)

Teachers from both year groups believed that children's learning of reading and writing benefited when they could copy more able peers, whether in pair work, group work or whole-class work. A couple of teachers described paired reading work, one of them in which Y4 children read with Y6 partners. Another described how,

> . . . those children who were more able . . . were able to work their way through the books they were reading . . . and the other children were actually getting the benefit of having a story read to them. They were seeing good reading behaviour, they were seeing how children worked out words they didn't know.

Children also gained good ideas and learned good learning behaviour from more able peers. This was especially useful in developing their story writing skills. Several teachers saw the necessity of poorer learners having access to the ideas of more able learners, particularly in group or whole-class settings, both at the beginning and the end of a session. A couple of teachers also described how a less able writer could learn by being paired with a more able writer:

> . . . I think with writing they can bounce off each other and my weakest writer can really enjoy working with my best writer, not doing the same work but sitting along side as a role model.

Paired writing could help both partners:

> They read each other's work and they are supposed to try and find something they could advise that person to do to make their work even better. Or it could be to point out something that they have missed.

g) Children learn through being critical of their own work

At least two-thirds of the teachers in our sample told us they believed that children's learning benefited when children were encouraged to be critical of their own work. In particular, they felt that children's self-checking skills were important within learning. Some teachers suggested that such self-checking or self-evaluation meant children comparing their work to specified targets; others saw it as meaning that children recognised their shortcomings and others again perceived it in terms of children acknowledging how much progress they had made. Most of teachers' references to children's skills in self-evaluation related to the learning of writing.

> Now that they are getting to the end of Year 2, we are helping them to be more self-critical and just things like checking the work, re-reading the work before saying they have finished it and you say, 'You spot the things you need to work on'.

(Y2)

In this way, children began to internalise criteria for good writing performance so that when they showed their work to the teacher, the criteria the teacher used to evaluate it were understood by the pupil too. This helped children to rely on their own judgements and take on independent responsibility for their own learning. Sometimes the teacher directed the child to the area of his or her work which needed special checking, for example, punctuation or leaving spaces between words. A Y6 teacher described how she '. . . *challenged some of them to say if they had forgotten the capital letter*' and she went on to comment, '*I think on every occasion they were able to find out what it was they needed to use to put it right'*.

One Y6 teacher stuck children's marked work on the classroom wall and asked children to deduce why she valued one piece of work more than another, using specified criteria for good performance. Similarly, another Y6 teacher told children which national curriculum level she had assessed their work to be at, and asked the individual child to decide whether it was the most appropriate level or not. In these ways, children were practising using the standards by which their own work was to be assessed, and this, we know, is a crucial aspect of developing the self-evaluating skills of a good learner.

Several teachers used the technique of asking children to look back through their exercise books and take note of how they had, or had not, improved, as the first step towards recognising how they should move forward. Alternatively, the teacher might ask children to be critical about how much they had learnt or achieved on any one day, again using their own individual standards against which to measure their learning or achievement.

h) Children learn when they initiate their own learning

It became clear from the interviews that the great majority of our teachers wanted children to become agents in their own learning, to have a degree of independence in their learning and to avoid relying on the teacher at all times to structure their learning. Twenty-one teachers mentioned that they wanted children to '*use their initiative*'; '*take the learning on for themselves*'; '*go off and plan their own thing that they want to make or do*'. The belief was that children can learn by themselves and in developing as learners should become increasingly able to pose questions for themselves, make links with other learning and be interested to pursue some line of research.

Teachers tried to encourage this in children firstly by providing them, through teaching, with basic skills then, for example, setting research for homework, giving children personal books to write in whenever they wanted, setting work which demanded that children selected their own equipment and resources. For example, in a Y2 classroom, the teacher had pinned up words around the room for the children to find and use in their stories and she explained: '*I like them to have an attempt themselves*'. A distinctive maths scheme, followed in one LEA by a number of Y6 teachers, was designed so that children could organise their own work and one of the teachers explained that the children '*know what they are doing and get on with it themselves*', while another reported: '*When they use* [the scheme], *they organise their own work, they collect their own cards, their own worksheets, their own materials. They go into the library, they use the tapes, they find partners to work on some of the cards*'.

Similarly, many Y6 teachers gave children the opportunity to devise their own tests in science rather than demonstrating an experiment and asking children to replicate it. Another example of children taking responsibility for their progress was when they set their own targets. A Y2 teacher explained:

> They are taking this on for themselves – if they set a target, there is an incentive for them to meet that target and to come back with the joy of meeting it and asking me to test them. If the target is spelling or a little aspect of maths . . . it helps them to learn, it gives them confidence and improves their self esteem.

A belief in developing independent learners influenced teachers' use of time and the way in which they organised the curriculum. For example, one Y2 teacher allowed some time for children to follow up work in a free way – there was a slot once a week when they could express their understanding through writing, drawing, model making and so on. It was their choice. Other teachers gave time to listening and discussing information children had brought from home (from the Internet, or books) when they had carried out some independent research on something the class were learning about. Able children were often challenged to take work further, with less input from the teacher.

Children's less conscious learning strategies

Over the course of our research teachers talked about less conscious ways of learning. They specifically mentioned '*thinking*', '*building up knowledge step by step*', and by '*making connections*'.

i) Children learn by thinking

It seems rather simplistic to say that teachers believed children learned by 'thinking' but it was strongly argued that thinking was a learning strategy not always used to the best advantage by children. More than one teacher suggested that children in general prefer not to think and feel happier and safer when they are told what to do by the teacher. However, the majority believed that children could (and should) be stimulated to think. All 24 teachers felt some responsibility to develop children's thinking and to make children more conscious of different types of thinking so they could better reason, solve problems and make deductions. Some talked about *'pushing children's thinking'* by *'always getting them to think about something on the next level up'*, *'something that little bit harder'*.

Teachers mentioned the loose term 'thinking' over and over again but also referred, on occasion, to the specific processes of: hypothesising (guessing, anticipating, speculating, predicting), 'working things out' (using and applying knowledge and understanding to problems) and 'reflecting' (pondering over something learned or evaluating one's learning strategies).

All teachers were keen to encourage children to hazard a guess or risk a prediction because this was the kind of thinking required in maths and science investigations. However the whole process of 'investigation' was described by at least two Y6 teachers as being extremely problematic for children because it depended on the ability to pose 'what if?' questions and the ability to understand that there was no one 'correct' solution. It was pointed out by several teachers that children were not always good at asking 'what if?' questions off their own bat and teachers felt compelled to model the type of questions children could ask.

> *I would pose a question in such a way that it leads them to think: 'What would you do?' 'What if you did it this way?'.*

and

> *Say, a maths investigation . . . it might be . . . Can you possibly find anything else out? Or is that the only answer? Or is that the only way of doing it?*

> *'Working things out for themselves', involves a range of thinking skills, unravelling and interpreting problems and applying what they already know. They have got to tussle with it because they have got to start to develop the intellectual skills to do it on their own.*

> (Y6)

If you just tell them what triangular numbers are, they are not learning anything, but if they work it through and find a pattern, and they have found it for themselves, they will remember it.

(Y2)

Maths and science were the two areas in which teachers thought children should be challenged to think in this way.

A few mentioned that conscious reflection was an important aspect of learning; reflection in the sense of pondering over something already learned as well as in the sense of analysing the success of one's own methods and strategies. A debriefing or rounding off time at the end of a lesson was the time when they could invite children to reflect on the lesson and on their own progress.

I think that when they come back at the end of the session, they need to reflect on what they have actually learnt, on what they have been doing and why they have been doing it and what they can now do better than they have been doing before.

(Y2)

j) Children learn by building up knowledge step by step

Many of the teachers expressed a belief (which was probably more commonly held) that children learned by building on what they already knew, building up knowledge step by step. The theory was that new skills were easily assimilated when previous knowledge was secure. Frequently teachers referred to *'learning the basics'* or *'learning the foundations'* before moving on. One example was that children need to have good spoken language before they can begin to get a notion that books contain speech written down.

Teachers were most likely to say that maths was a subject which children learned by building up steps. On the subject of maths, *'I think with maths it is very important that they have done the basics: sorting, matching, those activities before they are anywhere near ready to count.'* (Y2) *'One thing that comes to mind is fractions. Until they have had a lot of practical work with folding and recognising halves and quarters, they cannot go on'.* (Y6)

It was suggested by teachers of both age groups that, when learning the four rules of number, there were several stages ('important stepping stones') that children must pass through before being able to understand the next. It was emphasised that *'the lack of knowledge of one thing can prevent you from learning something else'.*

One outcome of a belief in step-by-step learning was that teachers pitched the level of tasks differently for different learners. Another was the use of graded maths schemes and school schemes of work based on a linear progression through subjects. The impact on pupil organisation was in some cases to 'set' by ability for maths (Y6) and reading (Y2).

k) Children learn by making connections

The third unconscious process that teachers identified was 'linking ideas' or 'making connections' and this of course was a key finding of the research we described in the first chapter. Teachers theorised that learning requires any learner to make connections – to link ideas together. One theory was that children learned to see 'the whole picture' by making connections between different aspects of the same subject. An example given was young children making the link between sounds and the written word. A Y2 teacher explained how she had modelled the formation of a particular set of letters on the blackboard, asked the children to 'shadow' write in the air while she did this, emphasised and repeated the phonic sounds in the letters being demonstrated and showed where these sounds appeared in a set of key words to be learned as weekly spellings. In this way she invited children to process and link elements of reading and writing simultaneously. A Y6 teacher explained that she took every opportunity to encourage children to develop a broader view of maths by connecting textbook learning about numbers or shapes to things all around them; by finding maths in the environment. The idea that children could come to understand something more easily if they connected ideas from 'real life' to school learning was common and influenced practice. Invariably, teachers would, in introductions to lessons, invite children to draw on their life experience and tell what they knew about any given subject, then explain the relevance of the child's contribution to the topic being studied, often weaving the child's contribution into the next part of teaching. Teachers also encouraged children to 'bring in bits and pieces from home' as they believed that learning was promoted if topics had relevance to children's own lives. Teachers also endeavoured to present children with 'real' tasks. For example, a Y6 teacher, instead of giving a worksheet of examples on percentages, gave children a mail order catalogue and a hypothetical sum of money to spend and set them off to work out discounts on goods of their own choice. Overall, teachers believed that it was their responsibility to point out links for children so that they would better use the brain's natural tendency to make connections.

THE CHILDREN'S VIEW OF LEARNING

When we spoke to the children we did not ask them to define 'learning', but it became obvious that they understood 'learning' to mean the acquisition of skills, knowledge or understanding. Skills that they learned were either 'how to do' or 'what to do' skills, with little differentiation in some younger children's minds between the two. For them, learning to carry out the teacher's instructions was as important as learning how to write. Some seven-year-olds perceived learning as making progress in skills already acquired in a basic form; for example, writing faster, spelling better, reading more fluently, doing harder sums. For nearly all the Y2 children, 'learning' meant possessing the 'right' knowledge or information. It was associated with finding the 'right' answer, some-times in test conditions; it meant correctly solving the problem set by the teacher. 'Learning' also meant having understanding, including being 'intelligent' or 'brainy'. However, the understanding these children were aiming for embraced personal and social understanding rather than being limited to, for example, understanding of concepts in the National Curriculum. They described how they learned to be patient; to settle arguments; not to be too noisy; not to 'show off too much'; learned how to be safe physically; learned to talk; also learned about how other people behave.

On the whole, the Y6 children we interviewed saw themselves as having personal responsibility for their own learning. They were also concerned about emotional safety to express misunderstandings and to be supported in their learning without ridicule. Learning for them could involve struggle and talking was an important process.

Children's learning strategies: the children's view

The learning strategies and processes that children described related to their own perceptions of 'learning'. The range of strategies covered by children was quite wide: thinking, visualising, remembering, memorising, talking and asking, listening, doing/handling, observing, reading, practising. Many of these, though not all, overlapped with what the adults thought.

a) Thinking

One learning process mentioned very frequently by the younger children was thinking, or using their brains, including concentrating and having to come up with new creative ideas. Sometimes 'thinking' was contrasted with using equipment, as if the brain and the practical were separate ways of learning. One child described this:

> . . . sometimes I do things in my head and sometimes I do it with my fingers. So I have to think and when I don't know and I can't do it with my fingers, like it's writing and I'm not quite sure . . . I have to think with my head and I go, 'Ah, I've got it!' So I really thought hard.

Some of the older children described 'imagining' and 'empathising' and these forms of thinking were useful in learning history, as one child explained 'you understand how people must have felt'. 'Interpreting the teacher's instructions' was another type of thinking articulated by older children – in all subjects this kind of thinking led to being able to apply something that had been taught. 'Solving' was another process described by the Y6 children. Solving for one boy consisted of:

> working out different ways of doing a mathematical problem by just looking at number sequences and thinking.

and for a girl:

> pouring concentration in, trying and struggling, you can get somewhere.

b) Visualising/remembering/memorising

Both Y6 and Y2 children described the strategy of visualising. One older boy explained that he used this regularly in mathematics to get the answers. He conjured up pictures in his mind, for example, visualising a cake divided into sections to help him with fractions.

Younger children found visualisation helpful to internalise learning material. One boy said he could visualise hundreds and thousands but not millions: to learn millions 'You'd have to write up all the numbers'. The younger children's stress on the usefulness of visualisation was linked to their recognition that learning involved a lot of remembering. One child connected the two by saying that children learn if '. . . they listen hard and look at the board and remember things . . . then they will remember them and they will be intelligent'. Y6 children did not name 'remembering' as a learning strategy but rather cited 'memorising'. 'Storing things in the mind' was essential for 'recalling things when you need to'.

c) Talking and asking

Older children were very conscious of the place of verbal interactions in learning. Asking questions of the teacher was described as a way of finding out something new or a way of confirming one's own thinking. Being asked questions made you use your brain and often clarified things in your mind. 'Just saying what you think' or answering the teacher's questions prompted the teacher to give feedback ('tell you whether you are on the right track'). Asking friends was described as a way of hearing an easier explanation while talking one-to-one with the teacher was a way of seeking clarification as well as personal feedback on progress. Joining in a discussion and talking with others revealed different ways of tackling a problem. ('Often you have an idea together that might just work'). Debating was seen as a useful way of hearing other people's opinions and learning new facts. Several children found brainstorming in groups helped them to 'connect ideas together'.

Younger children did describe learning through talking, but they did not share the Y6 children's belief in learning through discussion. Where talking was important, it usually entailed one-to-one interaction with the teacher or other adult. For younger children, talking was a means to clarifying a given point rather than an exploration of ideas.

d) Listening

Listening to the teacher was seen as a learning strategy by both age groups. For eleven-year-olds, it was especially important when the teacher was introducing something unfamiliar such as new and difficult concepts in maths, new spellings and aspects of punctuation, the names of parts of a flower or new facts in history and geography. Listening was equally important when the teacher was explaining how to go about a task or how to set work out.

One aspect of listening mentioned over and over again by the older children was 'eavesdropping' – listening in when the teacher was explaining to others. Eavesdropping clarified puzzling questions and sometimes yielded tips on how to tackle problems. As with brainstorming, 'listening – and discussing' as a combined learning strategy was instrumental in making connections between ideas. As one child expressed it 'by taking part, things come back to you'. The Y2 children emphasised strongly the importance of listening to the teacher and, generally, they imparted a sense of needing to receive information and instructions from the teacher in almost a passive way.

e) Doing/handling

Many Y6 children explained that being active and having hands-on experiences activated their thoughts and led to deeper understanding. For example, they described how experimenting, testing and *'getting the feel of materials'* allowed them to make estimations, guess at outcomes and see if predictions were correct; how *'having a touch of what it's like'*, and *'having a little fiddle with things'* helped them to analyse how things work. One explained that the beauty of doing experiments was discovery: *'you're not expecting something and suddenly it happens!'*.

Most of the Y2 children felt that access to equipment made it easier to reach answers; for this reason, some felt they no longer needed it much, only for new and difficult subjects. They most often referred to mathematics counting apparatus, and several expressed a preference for using their fingers or just their brains now that they were in Y2 and reasonably competent in basic number work: *'I don't really like using multi-link cubes . . . because it really gives the answer away very quickly.'* In contrast, using maths apparatus for counting was reported to be still quite useful by some members of Y6 – manipulating the equipment improved their concentration.

Other physical and kinaesthetic ways of learning mentioned by our interviewees were miming and acting, playing with new equipment and the physical act of writing things down which was a useful revision strategy.

f) Observing

Some eleven-year-olds explained that *'observing really carefully'* was a way of learning about scientific processes and the behaviour of different materials. 'Looking' and 'inspecting' were illuminating strategies: watching the teacher do demonstrations, examining diagrams and other data displays, or *'just seeing something written down'*. Outside the classroom, *'observing other people in your family and how they do things'* offered models for some Y6 children.

g) Reading

Reading as a means of gaining new information was mentioned by many older children, while only a few Y2 children rated reading books as a way of learning.

h) Practising

The idea of practising as a way of learning was more common to Y2 children's discussion. Many of them were clear about the benefits of regularly 'sitting down and doing it'. One child explained that:

> You learn for yourself the real meaning, because you find out for yourself . . . If you do it for yourself, if anybody ever asks you, you can always do it.

CONDITIONS FOR LEARNING: THE TEACHERS' VIEWS

As well as learning strategies and approaches, conditions for learning are an important aspect. Teachers talked a lot about the conditions or circumstances for children's learning. The children also talked about this, with some fervour, and it was something which we could see was important from our observations.

a) Children learn when they feel motivated

All the teachers believed that children learned when they felt motivated.

> All learning is linked to motivation . . . If children are desperate to learn, they will attain. It's not that they can't learn something, but they need to be motivated all the time. Then they need to feel a sense of achievement in order to want to learn.
>
> (Y6)

Teachers described the motivated child using the following terms: stimulated; challenged; encouraged; excited; tempted; enthused; wanting to learn; willing to try new things; interested; and inspired. They believed that children would learn when they felt one of these and it was the teacher's job to inspire these feelings, through a variety of means.

About one in four teachers told us they believed that external rewards motivated children to learn.

> . . . quality of work really does improve and quality of behaviour, because they are not just rewarded for their academic prowess, they are rewarded for being responsible individuals, caring individuals.
>
> (Y6)

Teachers mentioned incentives such as stars, smiley faces, credits, and house points. In one Y2 class, the children were motivating their own learning about punctuation by rewarding themselves with a counter if they got a complete sentence with full stop and capital letter. In addition, a few teachers mentioned that children were motivated to please the teacher in a general way, for example, by volunteering to help her during a lesson.

Again, feedback was important: talking in the context of Y2 children, one teacher said, '*Some are still struggling. If you don't give them any verbal feedback, I don't think they'd bother to try*'. Positive feedback could also be seen as a reward for good work and could help the child to see that the teacher was pleased with a specific aspect of his or her work. One Y2 teacher believed that children needed '*reassurance and praise in order to be willing to try new things*'. This aspect of motivation was connected to teachers' belief in the importance of children having enough self-esteem and confidence even to be able to respond to praise. Some children had more than others and those with less confidence needed more positive feedback to be motivated to learn. One Y6 teacher, for example, described how one child '*. . . needs a pat on the back every time he writes a sentence*', in order to be motivated to write the next.

Certain environmental or physical factors could assist teachers in motivating children to learn. One Y6 teacher described how the ethos and culture of a whole establishment helped children to achieve '*. . . because they are being given stimulus and excitement*'. Another stressed the value of '*. . . a stimulating environment, somewhere they want to go every day*'. She went on to say, '*I think display, your kind of workshop environment, is very important because it does affect their mood and their enthusiasm*'. A Y6 teacher used different methods of presenting creative writing lessons to keep children interested. She believed '*. . . if the lessons are interesting and they are in a stimulating and safe environment, they will want to know*'. A Y2 teacher believed that inviting children to present stories '*. . . with different tools and different equipment*' kept their interest in an otherwise difficult task. Partly because of the teacher's influence over children's feelings, as acknowledged by several teachers, some teachers believed it was important that the teacher herself was a motivated learner in their classroom. One Y6 teacher said, '*the teacher needs to "sell things" to children, to enthuse, encourage and motivate. If the teacher is enthusiastic, the children become enthusiastic*'. Another commented that '*If the teacher is not lively and enthusiastic, then the children will take that on*'.

One of the most powerful motivators in the view of several teachers was, however, task interest itself: if children found a task engaging and meaningful, they were more likely to work hard at it. This process was vividly expressed by one Y6 teacher:

> . . . I would usually start with a bang with a new concept, they sit up and take notice and a licking of the lips and relishing the prospect of this knowledge . . . You are like tempting them . . .

A Y2 teacher described how she tried to give children writing tasks such as writing a letter to a real person, writing a shopping list, writing a menu, or writing instructions on how to do something which would be more motivating than writing an imaginary story.

There was also a need for clear goals:

> . . . [target setting] can be motivation for the children who aren't motivated, the ones that can't be bothered anyway: if you set them a target, it gives them something to aim for.
>
> (Y2)

One reason teachers saw for encouraging individual target setting was that when a child achieved the target, he or she felt a sense of pride which motivated the child to achieve more.

> If you've got a target to aim towards and you meet it, you get a sense of achievement out of that and how you can proceed forward. It is very important that children see that too. I think that you have got to celebrate when targets are met as well.
>
> (Y6)

In a more general way, several teachers asked children to notice what they had learnt and to recognise this as an achievement.

b) Children learn when they feel safe to take risks

Nearly all the teachers we worked with believed that children learned when they felt safe to take risks; again, this was also felt strongly by the children. One of these teachers, a Y2 teacher, explained that children's learning was inhibited by:

> The child being frightened to fail or afraid of being criticised or afraid to try if they don't feel that their efforts are valued or they are ridiculed by their peers.

Y2 and Y6 teachers described what 'taking risks' meant for children and also what 'feeling safe' consisted of. They then told us which teaching strategies they believed could help children to feel safe and to take risks, so that, eventually, children would learn.

Teachers believed that children needed to feel confident doing something on their own initiative, without having to worry what they were allowed to do by the teacher. It was important that they felt able to take risks, 'have a go', and also to work independently of the teacher.

> . . . it is important for them to see that trying something out that you are not sure about is a perfectly acceptable way of working. You don't have to get things right all the time, you can try it out, you can say, 'I've worked at this, I've tried this idea, I've done what I can, but I feel I am not quite understanding this or that.'
>
> (Y6)

A very important aspect of taking risks was not minding making mistakes or failing in a task. One Y2 teacher told her class '. . . it's OK to make mistakes. That way you discover where you have gone wrong'.

Another essential aspect of taking risks was children being able to say what they thought and ask questions of, or discuss their problems with, the teacher. A Y6 teacher believed children needed to know that

> . . . I am on their side. If they have got a problem, it is OK to talk about it, it is all right to ask questions about something . . .

It was particularly Y6 teachers who stressed the need constantly to show children that risk taking was part of learning and that they would not get into trouble for taking risks and making mistakes; indeed one Y6 teacher believed teachers should praise risk taking more than praising correct answers. Another Y6 teacher stressed in science investigations that not having correct answers straight away was

> . . . the way that all scientists, even top scientists, learn: by observing, questioning, revisiting and questioning again.

There were two important strategies for encouraging children to risk giving their own answers. Teachers believed that if they showed that they listened to and valued all contributions, then children would learn to trust their own solutions to problems. In addition, if teachers did not suggest that they were the ultimate authority on all topics, children would feel like participants in a genuine learning enquiry.

> As long as children feel safe in the environment and are given opportunities, encouraged, shown in how to think through talking, feel safe in that, then they are quite happy to use their own initiative in learning.
>
> [Y2 teacher]

Several teachers also believed that the way in which teachers encouraged risk taking was very important. They stressed that the teacher had to be sensitive to the children's fears, patient with their sometimes incorrect suggestions, yet careful not to put children under pressure by intervening too much or moving too fast. One Y6 teacher's words encapsulated this belief when she said how vital it was

> . . . to make the children feel that I am not going to go on to the next thing until I have heard what they have got to say and I have got time and I will make time. No pressure.

A couple of teachers perceived that it was hard for some children to ask the teacher questions while other children were listening, for example in a whole-class situation. One Y6 teacher kept time apart specifically for children to be able to come and ask him questions about their mathematics, on a one-to-one basis.

An important part of this 'feeling safe' entailed the child feeling comfortable. They felt that it was very important that children had no fear of the teacher, or of being humiliated by the teacher or other pupils. A couple of teachers stressed that to feel safe, children needed to trust their teacher. For example, one Y6 teacher explained that it was essential that:

> . . . they don't feel worried or intimidated by the person who is teaching them, because that does happen: children feel bullied . . . they are frightened to say anything.

In addition, teachers of the younger children believed that children felt safe when they had acquired a certain basic competence in a learning area, whether it was confidence in number, confidence as a reader, confidence in spelling simple words correctly or confidence in using the computer.

It was predominantly Y6 teachers who told us that developing a particular classroom atmosphere was very important for making the child feel safe. One teacher summed the belief up by saying the classroom should be for the child:

> . . . *a place that he or she can be comfortable, with other children around for support. The atmosphere of the classroom is probably the most essential thing in helping or hindering learning.*

Teachers believed, therefore, that it was important for the teacher to build up a good relationship between them and pupils. It was also essential to set clear parameters or boundaries for learners, which provided some routine and security within which children could learn. One aspect of these boundaries included the teacher's expectations: if she made these clear from the outset, children would feel safer when learning.

CONDITIONS FOR LEARNING: THE CHILDREN'S VIEWS

Both Y6 and Y2 children described conditions that they believed were conducive to learning. They talked about the learner's physical state, frame of mind, attitude, age and ability. They also talked about 'classroom' conditions including teaching strategies and classroom climate.

'Learner' conditions

Eleven-year-olds explained that in order to learn it is important to be alert, not tired generally nor drained from a previous lesson which may have been difficult. It would be less easy to learn '*if you were stressed or had something on your mind such as a music exam after school*'. Similarly, part of feeling in a good state for learning for Y2 children was not feeling exhausted and not having too much on your mind: '*If you are grumpy then you don't really want to do anything, just want to lie down*'.

The older children noted the importance of '*being in the mood*' to learn, explaining that children learn better '*when the brain's in gear*' when they are able to concentrate and are '*not drifting off into space, thinking of the break up of the Spice Girls*' or '*that goal scored at playtime*'. Like Y6 children, several Y2 children voiced the importance of being '. . . *in a happy mood*' for learning and explained the need for the learning task to be enticing. One child expressed it:

> *. . . if I ever went to a strict school, I would never ever want to go there again because they are teaching me in this school that learning is fun and I think that is true . . .*

Both Y2 and Y6 children believed that, if they were enjoying a lesson, they learned more, whereas if they were bored they were liable to be easily distracted.

Older children stressed that the learner needs to feel confident about learning and about asking the teacher for help. Many appreciated talking to the teacher alone as it could be embarrassing to express a lack of understanding in front of classmates. As one girl expressed it:

> *It is nice if you can ask them things when they are with you, not when they are up in front of the class. So if you are really behind, to save everyone, like, knowing, it's nicest with just you and the teacher.*

The older children also raised the idea of having the right attitude to learning: 'you need to want to learn, be willing to try and be determined to do good work'. There is no point in thinking 'I won't be able to do it' nor in being over complacent, thinking 'Oh, this is easy'.

On subject of age, some eleven-year-olds believed that younger children could learn some of the same things as themselves:

> *Doesn't matter how young you are, it just depends how good you are at working, practising and doing revision.*

> *Age doesn't matter, some younger children are really into things and like a challenge.*

Others believe that younger children couldn't learn the same things because 'when you are older you are able to understand the teacher more easily, you can take more in' or because 'learning has to be step-by-step; you need to learn some stuff to be able to cope with harder stuff'. Most of the seven-year-olds agreed that there were some things they were too young to learn although they felt they could sometimes be pushed to learn more. They thought that you had to be old enough to learn certain hard skills, such as doing sums with big numbers and reading long words. One or two Y6 children theorised that all children, regardless of age, use the same ways of learning despite the level of difficulty of work.

All the children interviewed were conscious that some children are of a higher academic ability than others, this meant doing work at difficult levels, and they expressed trust in their teachers to pitch work at the right level.

Classroom conditions

The older children believed that classroom ethos was a crucial factor in promoting learning and described a relaxed and happy environment as well as:

> a class where arrangements are set up to raise your self esteem – not make you feel you are nothing.

The Y2 children did not talk about a classroom ethos in the way the Y6 children did. The Y2 children emphasised that for learning, they needed constant access to help, preferably through one-to-one interaction with the teacher which sometimes meant the teacher simply giving them an answer. This implied that when the teacher was teaching from the front of class, it was harder for them to learn. They preferred a small group in that:

> . . . the person who is really stuck on the hard sum could say, 'Can you help me with this?' and somebody says, 'Is it a times sum?' and they say, 'Yes', and they teach them their times table in a strong kind of way.

The help they needed could come from other children in the group or from classroom helpers:

> If you are writing something with say another teacher, like a helper, it's better because you don't have to do everything at once or all by yourself and it would be easy.

Several younger children said they needed quietness for learning. They could not listen if other children were making a noise, and so they could not learn. One child summed it up:

> Children learn by their being in a quiet spot and thinking as hard as you can and you could get like really good at things.

Eleven-year-olds mentioned teaching strategies which helped them learn. They liked it when the teacher gave or allowed introductory, warm-up activities that helped them 'get ready to learn', such as: playing with a Rubik cube first thing in the morning, mental arithmetic problems during registration, a story before starting work after playtime. They appreciated a revision of something previously taught at the beginning of lessons and welcomed explicit information such as '*your teacher tells you when it's going to be a new thing*'. A teaching strategy found to be helpful during maths was described as '*when the teacher calls people out and asks them to show the way they did something*'. In English, helpful strategies were '*when the teacher feeds back to the class good ideas, middle ideas and ideas that are not quite right*'.

Children of both age groups described organisational arrangements, which helped them to learn. Older children believed that seating should be arranged so that everyone could easily see and hear the teacher's demonstration or introduction and one Y2 child commented that children who sat at the back of class did not learn to spell as well as those near the board at the front. (This was linked to their view that the blackboard was helpful for learning).

To maximise individual learning in a group situation, Y6 children considered it important that the group was not too large: '*possibly five with sufficient equipment to go round*', was one child's suggestion. They believed mixed ability groups were better than ability groups because there was '*usually someone who could help you*'. They explained that they learned more if they were paired with '*someone on one's own level or sometimes that little bit better*'. They learned best when: routines were consistent and familiar; they were allowed plenty of time to do things; work was pitched to be just achievable; and that there was only one key thing to be learned at any one time.

CONCLUSIONS

Both teachers and children had a lot to say about learning. While these 'expert' teachers did not allow particular learning theories to guide their practice directly, we found that they **do** hold beliefs about how children learn, and the strategies they used were based on these beliefs. Drawing together their beliefs about learning styles, motivation, interaction, and children's thinking with the strategies we saw them use, we can say that these 'expert' teachers do indeed base their teaching on understandings of learning. For example, interview data indicates a belief that individuals learn in different ways. Teachers did not refer directly to the work of authors such as Howard Gardner (1991), yet they were observed to use a strategy we named as 'giving different treatment' (differentiating the task, using different type of feedback and tone of voice, pitching different questions at different levels for different children, and suggesting different equipment for different children) trying to present a way of teaching to reach everyone. Activity (hands-on experience and use of aids, experiments, making things and practising, rather than 'busy work') was a key theme; as was making connections, relating new to existing information, encouraging the children to think and to think for themselves.

Teachers believe children learn through a combination of different learning strategies (by listening, 'doing', finding out for themselves, practising, thinking alone, copying others and talking and discussing with others). Thus, in response to the 'dilemma' addressed by formal theory 'Is learning located in the head or in the individual-in-social-action?', the answer was consistently that learning happens in both ways. This belief led the teachers to use a range of organisational and teaching strategies, and to set up conditions for independent and collaborative learning. (Vygotsky's (1978) view, of course, was that learning occurs twice: first as social interaction and then as internalisation.) The belief that children's learning is helped by a combination of different teaching strategies underpins the wide repertoire of teaching, assessment and feedback methods we saw the teachers use.

At times, the children's thinking also resonated with theories of learning. For example, constructivist ideas were echoed in the children's responses about listening-and-discussing as a combination which fostered the connection and association of ideas and led to problem solving. The apprenticeship approach was echoed in the children's experience of learning from role models in the family. Younger children constantly referred to the teacher as transmitter of information while the discourse of both age groups was peppered with references to active learning. In the children's responses there were traces of thinking about 'readiness' and sequential development: some believed they could attempt anything while others believed in having to learn some things before others.

The seven-year-olds were still acquiring basic skills and mastery of these demanded much of their attention. This was possibly why they were so aware of progress within these skills. On the other hand, they also demonstrated a noticeably broad perception of learning, to include a social and physical understanding of their environment. By Y6 the children were better able to reflect upon their skills, knowledge and understanding. They demonstrated an appreciation of the role of talk in learning and were beginning to articulate their own mental processes.

It is probably true that the younger children responded to our interviews with specific recent learning experiences in mind, while the older children could better abstract and generalise. What is interesting, however, is that even the youngest children were mirroring some of the thinking about learning of secondary school students, as we discuss in the final chapter.

Chapter 7

Synthesis

In the preceding chapters we have described the lesson patterns, teaching, assessment and feedback strategies of the 'expert' primary teachers in the study. We also described how they, and the pupils, talked about learning in the classroom.

We now want to look at how the activities are linked, the impact of the age difference, whether what we found is supported by any other research, and what are for us the key issues.

PATTERN AND SEQUENCE

What can we say about the links among the strategies and the pattern of use? **The same strategies were repeatedly used at the same stage in lessons and with the same audiences.**

Teachers typically used informing and scaffolding strategies in lesson introductions (all subjects) when they worked with the whole class before activities. These introductions were interactive, the aim being to motivate the learners. When children were working on activities, teachers regularly toured the room spreading their attention across individuals. This was the prime context for: checking and observing (allowing teachers to gauge the level of individual or group progress on a task) and for re-demonstrating (when teachers repeated teaching). Not surprisingly, teachers also tended to 'specify a better way of doing something' when children were working on activities. This seemed particularly fitting because children could act immediately on the feedback. By drawing the whole class together in a plenary context at the end, teachers were able to summarise what had been achieved or not achieved and sometimes repeat teaching through the strategies of re-demonstration, reminding children of key knowledge, conveying examples of children's work and describing why answers were correct.

Particular strategies were regularly used in particular types of lesson

'Telling children what they have or have not achieved' was often used at the beginning of a lesson of practising skills. Teachers summarised what had already been achieved but also what children still needed to do. They were also inclined to get individuals to suggest ways in which they could improve during these lessons rather than during lessons where new knowledge was being presented because they could not expect improvement if a basic level of competence had not been reached. Teachers used this strategy particularly in the context of writing to get children to improve letter formation, punctuation and spelling.

Teachers reported more 'demonstrating' when a lesson in any subject involved the presentation of new knowledge. In contrast, when children were trying to 'apply' a method they had learned to a problematic task, too much teacher-demonstration was thought to be antithetical to learning.

'Explaining' was used more often when introducing new knowledge or understanding and least used when children were set investigative tasks in maths and science. In contrast, 'eavesdropping' was used uniquely when children were engaged upon investigative tasks in groups. Teachers stood in the wings and listened in to brainstorming, discussion, and task planning.

How did these teachers incorporate informal assessment and feedback to the learner into the teaching/learning cycle?

The feedback strategy of 'specifying or implying a better way of doing something' (showing how to make specific corrections, advising quicker or more successful methods) followed an assessment of a child's achievements commonly through the assessment strategies of 'observing' (watching closely) or 'getting children to demonstrate' how they had been doing something. Specifying a better way of doing something then implicated the teacher in using the teaching strategies of modelling, remodelling, and relaying learning strategies.

When teachers assessed by close observation, for example, a child carrying out a number operation or forming a letter, they frequently followed this by the feedback strategy of telling a child whether they were right or wrong and then by teaching, i.e. by 'instructing' step by step. This usually led on to 'directing children to further practice'.

'Oral testing' (quizzing, firing spot questions) as an assessment strategy was sometimes used with individuals about work after it had been completed. This was particularly the case in maths when children worked through a graded series of work cards. Oral testing was regularly followed by the feedback strategy of 'telling a child what they have or have not achieved', and then the teaching strategies of explaining and re-demonstrating.

Teachers used the assessment strategy of 'delving' to find out how individual children arrived at an incorrect answer (usually in maths and science). Delving involved a mixture of closed and more open-ended questions and was used in sustained interactions with individuals in which there were repeated instances of assessment-feedback-teaching. Delving made it necessary for the teacher to listen carefully to the child's responses, meaning that interactions involving delving were peppered with diverse feedback strategies, including detailing what a child had achieved, 'telling a child they were right or wrong' and 'specifying a better way of doing something'. Following each stint of assessment and feedback, different teaching strategies were brought into play according to need, such as relaying learning strategies, modelling and demonstrating.

At times verbal feedback was missing from the sequence and assessment was directly followed by teaching. For example: in the context of teachers touring the room when children were working on activities, the assessment strategies of 'checking' and 'observing' (noticing how children had begun to tackle a task) were ordinarily followed by the teaching strategies of 'giving instructions' or 'relaying learning strategies' through the teacher addressing the whole class. Teachers often omitted feedback when they were making (and recording) assessments against National Curriculum criteria (particularly speaking and listening, using and applying maths and experimental and investigative science). In this context, the assessment strategies of observing, listening and eavesdropping were usually followed on a later occasion by directing children to further practising or relaying (new) knowledge – moving on to a new topic.

At times, for example during the middle of maths lessons, when a child had completed one worksheet and was about to move on to the next, teachers would give spot questions (oral testing) on the content of the new sheet to judge whether the child had sufficient understanding to proceed. Assessment by oral testing in cases like this was followed either by 'directing to further practising' or directing to the next task.

Teachers typically used certain strategies alongside certain others

Although these expert teachers used extensive evaluative feedback (mostly, but not always, positive) their practice was also strongly characterised by descriptive feedback. Particular *feedback* strategies were used consistently in connection with particular teaching strategies, for example

Teachers used the feedback strategy of 'describing why an answer is correct' in connection with the teaching strategy: 'conveying examples of children's methods and work' which could involve teachers asking children to read out or describe examples. They described why one child's answer was good in order to confirm what was good about it and also to inform other children. On the whole, teachers used the feedback strategy of 'getting children to suggest ways they can improve' in connection with the teaching strategy of 'questioning to promote thinking' (for example, by asking *'What would make this better?'*)

Particular *assessment* strategies were used in association with particular *teaching* strategies, for example:

- 'Oral testing' and 'gauging the level' recurred alongside 'relaying knowledge' in the context of lesson introductions. Teachers picked up the general level of understanding of the class and used this to guide and structure their input of facts.

- 'Getting a child to demonstrate' was frequently used in association with 'relaying learning strategies'. Rarely did a teacher ask a child to show their ways of working without advising them of a better way of going about something.

- 'Oral testing' was used to recap previous knowledge at the beginning of lessons. It was regularly used alongside repeating children's correct answers and 'explaining' in order to emphasise and drive home a piece of knowledge or understanding.

WHAT ARE THE DIFFERENCES BETWEEN TEACHING SEVEN AND ELEVEN-YEAR-OLDS?

A common difference was in lesson pattern. The three-stage format with teaching a focus group in the middle stage was used more by Y2 teachers; the three-stage format with spreading attention in the middle stage was favoured by Y6 teachers; and the multi-stage lesson was observed *only* in Y6 classrooms. So, infant teachers tended to do intensive teaching of a group, with the other children working independently, while Y6 teachers worked more often with the whole class, sometimes in pacy lessons with a variety of tasks.

Apart from this, we found that the practice of these expert infant and junior teachers corresponded more than it differed. Where there were differences in *teaching,* junior teachers were more likely to 'relay ways of learning' while infant teachers gave more one-to-one re-demonstration, possibly because they were dedicated to giving children the basic skills.

Where there were differences in *assessment* junior·teachers made more use of standardised and teacher-designed tests; Y2 teachers were more likely to observe and then write an assessment note for themselves about a child's progress. Also, as more Y2 than Y6 teachers focused their attention intensively on one group when the children were working, some Y2 teachers were less likely to check on the whole class in the middle of lessons, although they carried out thorough checking on their focus group.

Where there were differences in *feedback* giving rewards played a more important role in infant than in junior classrooms, perhaps because teachers felt that children's self-esteem and confidence needed more boosting at the earlier age. Infant teachers questioned the usefulness of written feedback, because Y2 children could not read the comments. Y2 teachers were therefore less likely than Y6 teachers to give extensive written comments on children's work and preferred to tell children to come and discuss an area for improvement with them. From among our sample it was the Y6 teachers who most often used the feedback strategy of 'telling children what they had and had not achieved', typically in relation to writing tasks.

Both Y6 and Y2 teachers saw the importance of 'expressing approval' in order to show children they were valued as people and/or for their work. Although we might have expected infant teachers to stress the need for expressions of approval more than junior teachers, our data did not support this. Perhaps also surprisingly, teachers of younger as well as older children described getting children to be self-critical about their work and using discussion to provoke children's thoughts about how they could improve.

Although differences in practice of good infant and good junior teachers are fewer than the similarities, there does seem to be a shift from a focus on intensive teaching of individuals and small groups, assessment by a wide range of strategies (including making assessment notes to self on individual progress) and the use of feedback with an emphasis on building confidence in the learner, at Y2, to the approaches used in Y6. Here the focus is on more interactive whole-class teaching and communication about how to learn, assessment by a wide range of strategies (including an increase in written tests) and feedback (increasingly written down) on what had not been achieved in relation to what should have been achieved.

VALIDATION

Since our sample was quite small we have to ask how our findings resonate with the work of others. We can do this in relation to teaching, conditions for learning and the teacher-pupil relationship, by looking at published research.

Teaching

Rosenshine and Stevens (1986), summarising American research on effective teachers at primary level, found that generally in teaching 'well-structured' subjects they:

- begin a lesson with a short review of previous prerequisite learning;
- begin a lesson with a short statements of goals;
- present new material in small steps, with student practice after each step;
- give clear and detailed instructions and explanations;
- provide a high level of active practice for all students;
- ask a large number of questions, check for student understanding, and obtain responses from all students;
- guide students during initial practice;
- provide systematic feedback and corrections;
- provide explicit instruction and practice for seatwork exercises and, where necessary, monitor students during seatwork.

(1986 p. 377)

They argue that this approach is less applicable for teaching 'ill-structured' areas, i.e. where the skills to be taught do not follow explicit steps, involve creativity or intuition. We would say that we found much of this practice in relation to the lesson structure and teaching strategies of our teachers across the 'core' subjects of reading, writing, mathematics, and science at age eleven.

We pointed out in Chapter 1 that primary teachers were encouraged to use a teaching repertoire. It is not new to recognise that effective teachers have a repertoire of approaches. Arends (1991) argues that:

'Effective teaching requires as its baseline individuals who are academically able and who care about the well-being of children and youth'.

(1991 p. 6)

But, he argues, there need to be other attributes:

- control of a knowledge base that guides the art of teaching;
- a repertoire of best practices;
- the attitudes and skills necessary for reflection;
- the view that learning to teach is a life-long process.

Arends's view is that effective teachers have diverse repertoires and are not restricted to a 'few pet practices'. In the UK Brown and McIntyre (1993) similarly use the notion of a repertoire suggesting that: 'experienced and expert teachers

- arrive at the class with clear goals for the pattern of activity and for the progress to be made by the pupils;
- make rapid initial judgements about the conditions impinging on the teaching, based on

  a) cues which are evident on the occasion, and
  b) knowledge they already have about pupils, the environments, the curriculum and themselves;

- quickly select from their repertoire of actions those which their experience tells them are best suited to achieve their goals in the given conditions or alternatively modify or replace their goals.

(1993 p. 83)

There is no doubt that the teachers in the study described in this book had, and used, a wide-ranging repertoire, not just for teaching but also for assessment and feedback.

A recent review of research on student learning over the last 10 years (Hattie, 1999) found that: the most powerful single factor that enhances achievement is feedback; the setting of appropriate, specific and challenging goals is critical; and proposes that increases in student learning involve, not only surface and deep learning, but also the reconceptualisation of information.

Other studies have looked at good teaching in relation to thinking and learning. For example, Askew and colleagues (1997) found, in the research referred to in Chapter 1, that highly effective teachers of numeracy used teaching approaches which:

- connected different areas of mathematics;
- encouraged pupils to describe their methods and their reasoning, and used these for developing understanding and establishing connections;
- emphasised the importance of using mental, written or electronic methods of calculation that were the most efficient for the problem in hand.

They also believed in the importance of dialogue and shared imagery so that teachers gained better understanding of pupils' thinking and pupils gained access to the teachers' knowledge. These teachers used teaching approaches which encouraged discussion in whole classes, small groups, or with individual pupils. They used systematic assessment and recording methods to monitor pupils' progress and record their strategies for calculation, to inform planning and teaching. Less effective teachers either used little assessment or used it as a check that taught methods had been learned.

In the parallel study on the teaching of literacy, Medwell and colleagues (1998) found that effective teachers of literacy: generally placed a high priority on meaning in their teaching of literacy, centring much teaching around 'shared texts' as a means of making the connections between word, sentence and text explicit to the children; taught the conventions of reading and writing in a systematic and structured way but also in a way that made clear to pupils the reasons for their importance; tended to emphasize the functions of the language features they were teaching, e.g. learning the rules of grammar would help improve their writing; had well-developed systems for monitoring and assessment, using their findings in subsequent planning. Also

> The lessons of these teachers were conducted at a brisk pace. They regularly refocused children's attention on the task at hand and used clear time frames to keep children on task. They also tended to conclude their lessons by reviewing, with the whole class, what

the children had done during the lesson. Lessons which ended with the teacher simply saying 'We'll finish this tomorrow' were much more common among the validation [or control] teachers; the effective teachers also used modelling extensively. They regularly demonstrated reading and writing to their classes in a variety of ways, often accompanying these demonstrations by verbal explanations of what they were doing.

(1998 p. 78)

The findings of these two studies echo what we observed with our teachers: making purpose and content explicit; careful planning; systematic assessment and feedback; making connections; encouraging children to think and to think about thinking; modelling what they wished children to do.

Conditions for learning

An interesting aspect of our findings was teachers' and pupils' emphasis on conditions for learning. Much of the research has focussed on asking pupils about their attitudes to school and what makes a good teacher; information about conditions for learning tends to be a by-product.

For secondary pupils, 'good' teachers are ones who: present work in a way which interests and motivates pupils; provide conditions so pupils understand the work; make clear what pupils are to do and achieve; and help pupils with difficulties (Brown and McIntyre, 1993 pp. 28–29). They show some willingness to allow pupils to have input into goal and agenda setting; provide a supportive social context to help pupils feel accepted, cared for and valued; and take into account pupil circumstances and modify/pace/structure learning tasks accordingly. (Cooper and McIntyre, 1996). Rudduck reports that the pupils' view of what make good conditions for learning include: respect for pupils as individuals; fairness to all pupils irrespective of their class, gender, ethnicity or academic status; autonomy; intellectual challenge that helps pupils to experience learning as a dynamic, engaging and empowering activity (Rudduck, Chaplain and Wallace, 1996).

Cooper and McIntyre argue that when teachers and pupils focus on perceptions of teaching that leads to effective learning there is considerable overlap between their views including: a belief in the importance of the active involvement of pupils in the learning process; the teachers' willingness to make use of pupils' ideas and ways of thinking, in their own thinking about how to make new knowledge accessible;

an emphasis on encouraging pupils to construct and share their own understandings during lessons.

> ...a key issue ... is the extent to which teachers are willing to share with pupils control over lesson content and learning objectives, and that effective teaching (as defined by teachers and pupils in this study) often seems to depend on the form of power-sharing in these areas.
>
> (Cooper and McIntyre, 1996 p. 89)

At primary level, Pollard (1990) found that it was the ratio of risk to enjoyment that determined how children felt about tasks, rather than the nature of the tasks themselves. What children like best about their teacher is fairness and being able to explain things well (Wragg, 1993). A longitudinal study found that views varied across years and between genders but the issue of pupil autonomy kept emerging: pupils preferred not to be constantly controlled and directed. (This resonates with the findings of Rudduck et al. and Cooper and McIntyre above.) As they moved through the first two years of Key Stage 2 the pupils in Pollard and colleagues' study became increasingly aware of teacher power and were very aware of the extent to which their activities were evaluated by teachers (Broadfoot and Pollard, 1996). Their preferred orientation was pleasing the teacher rather than learning per se, and there was a growing preoccupation with avoiding failure (Broadfoot and Pollard, 1998).

In conclusion, the children in our study were as interested as those interviewed by Brown and McIntyre (op cit) in having clear information from the teacher and work presented in an exciting way; our children stressed active involvement and sharing their understandings with others (Y6) as did the respondents of Cooper and McIntyre. Our eleven-years-olds saw learning as their own responsibility and preferred not to be constantly controlled, as did the learners in other studies.

We also know from the work of psychologists and classroom researchers about the importance of classroom climate in enabling children to feel 'safe' and to take risks in learning. American psychologists Ames and Ames (1984) described how learning environments can be differentiated in terms of specific cues which influence the ways in which children process information and come to understand their performance. Their argument is that certain classroom structures can influence goal orientation in children. Positive structures include assessment (or evaluation) strategies which: focus on individual improvement, progress and mastery rather than comparison; make evaluation private, not public; recognise and reward student effort; provide opportunities for improvement; and encourage a view of mistakes as part of learning (Ames, 1992 p. 267).

Douglas Barnes, as early as 1976 wrote about the importance of equal status and mutual trust between teacher and pupil in order to allow and encourage risk taking (Barnes, 1976). In New Zealand, work with Maori pupils similarly constructs the notion of a 'safe' learning environment. This entails the good teacher respecting the moral and spiritual presence of the child, and boosting it, in order to encourage learning in the individual and a good class atmosphere. Such a teacher would deal with mistakes in a way that would not 'crush' the child or produce a negative atmosphere. (Airini, 1998). Similarly work in the USA on learning classrooms describes a community of learners which entails collaborative learning in a 'community of practice'. The collaboration promotes 'an atmosphere of joint responsibility, mutual respect, and a sense of personal and group identity' (Brown, 1994 p. 10). This, we felt was true of many of 'our' classes.

The teacher–pupil relationship

The relationship between teacher and pupil, which is a key aspect of classroom climate, can be illustrated clearly through assessment. Torrance and Pryor (1998) argue that informal assessment in the classroom can be construed as a key arena for the negotiation of classroom relationships and we would agree. They use the example of assessment of children aged five (on entry to the first stage of schooling) to show that it is by no means just an assessment activity but part of the child's earliest initiation into the rituals of schooling. While the teacher attempts to encourage the pupil's responses by praise, smiles etc., in their example she is also determined to exercise control over the pupil in order to accomplish her agenda.

Black and Wiliam (1998) also argue that the negotiation of classroom life will be determined by the beliefs of teachers and pupils about learning and power relations. When a teacher questions a student, the teacher's beliefs will influence both the questions asked and the way that answers are interpreted. In turn, the student's responses to questioning will depend on a host of other factors: whether the student believes 'ability' to be open to improvement or fixed, for instance, will have a strong influence on how the student sees a question – as an opportunity to learn (which involves taking a risk) or as a threat to self-esteem.

Teacher–pupil relationships in assessment are the subject of much debate (see Gipps, 1999) which may not seem relevant to the issues in this book. In traditional teaching the assessment relationship is directive and hierarchical: the teacher assesses and the pupils receive judgements. However, if teaching is aiming towards the development of good learning strategies in the pupil including the development of autonomy (taking some responsibility for one's own learning) and the ability to evaluate one's own work and progress (becoming a self-monitoring learner) then the teacher–pupil relationship needs to be more open and enabling, or constructing, than directing.

Royce Sadler whose work on formative assessment was described in Chapter 1, points out that teachers bring to the classroom a more elaborate and extensive knowledge base than their students, including: skill in assessments; a deep knowledge of criteria and standards appropriate to the assessment task; evaluative skill in making judgements about student performance, and expertise in framing feedback statements. Sadler argues that some of these skills need to be shared with students, because:

> ... ultimately the intention of most educational systems is to help students not only grow in knowledge and expertise, but also to become progressively independent of the teacher for lifelong learning. Hence if teacher-supplied feedback is to give way to self assessment and self monitoring, some of what the teacher brings to the assessment act must itself become part of the curriculum for the student, not an accidental or inconsequential adjunct to it ...
>
> (Sadler, 1998 p. 82)

This just as important for young learners as for older learners. But, in order to bring the student into some ownership of the learning and assessment process (and hence into self-evaluation and metacognition) it means teachers sharing power with students – rather than exerting power over them. This requires teachers to think about their relationships as, in both learning and assessment, they shift responsibility to the learner. This does *not* mean the teacher giving up responsibility for their pupils' learning and progress; far from it. It means that the teacher has to take on the added responsibility of involving the learner as a partner and doing so explicitly. If children are to become lifelong learners they need to be taught how to learn, and how to take control of their learning. Our findings on feedback show quite clearly how teachers can use the assessment process to support the learner and at the same time to encourage self-evaluation and self-direction.

Jerome Bruner (1996) argues that we need to move on from an impoverished conception of teaching

> in which a single, presumably omniscient teacher explicitly tells or shows presumably unknowing learners something they presumably know nothing about.
>
> (p. 20)

He writes instead of developing the classroom as a community of mutual learners:

> with the teacher orchestrating the proceedings. *Note that, contrary to traditional critics, such subcommunities do not reduce the teacher's role nor his or her 'authority'*. Rather, the teacher takes on the additional function of encouraging others to share it. Just as the omniscient narrator has disappeared from modern fiction, so will the omniscient teacher disappear from the classroom of the future.
>
> (Bruner, 1996 pp. 211–22, our emphasis.)

In many of the classrooms in which we worked there was a real sense of being in a learning environment, a community even, with learning as a purposeful, demanding and shared activity. The latter could not be achieved without a particular classroom ethos, built on a particular teacher–pupil relationship. In these classes children and teachers operated with clear understandings and mutual respect. The visits were, for us, heartening experiences where expert teachers were working with engaged and enthusiastic learners.

CONCLUSIONS: KEY ISSUES

The teaching, assessment and feedback strategies of these expert primary teachers were complex as was their deployment. The teachers had repertoires of strategies and employed them in a range of ways appropriate to the age of the learner, the subject being studied, and the teaching context. This much is already well understood in the literature. The most common lesson type was a three-stage format in which the teacher first relayed or reinforced information and then worked with groups, or monitored individuals, during the middle stage of the lesson just as in the literacy and numeracy hour. The 'expert' teacher is active and interactive; when pupils are set to groupwork or individual tasks the teacher does not sit and do marking, but works with the pupils. This too reflects findings of good practice from the evaluation of the introduction of the National Literacy Strategy (Ofsted, 1999).

What we emphasise now are some other findings which we believe are key issues.

First, the very complexity of the teacher's actions is in contrast to the clarity provided for the learner: clarity of task, goal, requirement, and most importantly clarity about progress made. The teachers used regular informal assessment strategies including a range of types of questioning, observation and listening-in. Their practice was characterised by regular feedback to the pupils about their methods of working and the content of their work. Thus, the teachers knew where the learners were and so did the learners. (The very antitheses of what Torrance and Pryor (1998) describe as a guessing game for the learner.) These teachers were adept at being constructive and encouraging while at the same time being realistic with children about their performance.

Second, there was a strong focus on each individual's learning; however, this did not involve working consistently with individuals as in common (mis)perceptions of progressive primary teaching in the Plowden days. It was, rather, an understanding that since individuals learn at different rates and in different ways teachers have to provide a variety of activities, tasks and pace of work, and constantly monitor and evaluate children's progress.

The third theme is learning itself. While the teachers did not refer to formal learning theory they did work on the basis of intuitive learning theories (which mapped on to a broad range of formal learning theory). Teaching – that is relaying information – is important, but children need to think, to make connections, to practise and reinforce, to learn from other learners, and to feel that if they make mistakes they will not be ridiculed or treated negatively. This notion that emotional safety is necessary for intellectual risk taking was echoed by the pupils. The importance of a classroom atmosphere in which it is acceptable (and safe) to make mistakes and take risks was made very clear. This resonates with the approach of the Learning to Learn initiative in which creating the optimal balance between high challenge and low threat in the classroom, and building in feedback, are seen to be crucial aspects of creating an effective learning environment (Lucas, 2000).

The younger pupils were also strongly aware that they needed dedicated teacher input for learning, preferably in a one-to-one or small group setting. Older pupils were happier to learn in collaborative groups while younger children found this hard to sustain. All the pupils valued using apparatus and doing active tasks in the process of learning.

Both the pupils and teachers were reflective about learning and both, also, talked about learning in different ways (in the head, through practical activity; alone, in a group; from the teacher, from home/the world outside, from other learners). The teachers gave short shrift to any notion that learning could be theorised in simple either/or ways: a social or a cognitive process; taking place in the head or in the individual-in-social-action. Learning is a far more complex process than this. This understanding of a range of ways of learning within and across learners underpinned their use of a complex range of strategies.

We hope that by describing the teaching, assessment and feedback strategies of these teachers, by describing their lesson patterns, by unpacking their beliefs and actions in relation to pupils' learning, (and that of the pupils) we have made a contribution to understanding the complex and diverse activity that makes up primary teaching. We hope, too, that we have helped to make clear some of the ground rules for teachers to teach so that children can learn.

Bibliography

Airini (1998) What is good teaching? Lessons from Maori pedagogy. Paper presented to NZARE Conference, December 1998, Dunedin, New Zealand.

Alexander, R., Rose, J. and Woodhead, C. (1992) *Curriculum Organisation and Classroom Practice in Primary Schools*. London, DES.

Alexander, R. J. (1995) *Task, Time, Talk and Text: Signposts to Effective Teaching?* International Conference on School Effectiveness and Learning Achievement at the Primary Level, New Delhi.

Ames, C. (1992) 'Classrooms: Goals, structures and student motivation', *Journal of Educational Psychology*, **84**, 3, pp. 261–71.

Ames, C. and Ames, R. (1984) 'Systems of student and teacher motivation: Toward a qualitative definition', *Journal of Educational Psychology*, **76**, pp. 535–56.

Arends R. I. (1991) *Learning to Teach*. New York, McGraw-Hill, 2nd edition.

Askew, M., Brown, M., Rhodes, V., Johnson, D. and Wiliam, D. (1997) *Effective Teachers of Numeracy*. Final Report to TTA, School of Education, King's College, London.

Barnes, D. (1976) *From Communication to Curriculum*. London, Penguin.

Black, P. and Wiliam, D. (1998) 'Assessment and classroom learning', *Assessment in Education*, **5**, 1, pp. 7–73.

Broadfoot, P. and Pollard, A. (1996) 'Continuity and change in English Primary Education' in Croll, P. (ed.) *Teachers, Pupils and Primary Schooling: Continuity and Change*. London, Cassell.

Broadfoot, P. and Pollard, A. (1998) Categories, standards and instrumentalism: Theorising the changing discourse of assessment policy in English primary education. Paper given to AERA Conference, San Diego, April 1998.

Brown, A. (1994) 'The Advancement of Learning', *Educational Researcher*, **23**, 8, pp. 4–12.

Brown, S. and McIntyre, D. (1993) *Making Sense of Teaching*. Milton Keynes, Open University Press.

Bruner, J. (1996) *The Culture of Education*. Massachusetts, Harvard University Press.

Bruner, J. and Haste, H. (1987) *Making Sense: The Child's Construction of the World*. New York, Routledge.

Cobb, P. (1994) 'Where is the mind?' *Educational Researcher*, **23**, 7, pp. 13–20.

Cooper, P. and McIntyre, D. (1996) *Effective Teaching and Learning*. Milton Keynes, Open University Press.

DfEE (1998) *The National Literacy Strategy*. London: HMSO.

DfEE (1998) *Teaching: High Status, High Standards: Requirements for courses of Initial Teacher Training Circular 4/98: Training*. London, HMSO.

Driver, R., Asoko, H., Leach, J., Mortimer, E. and Scott, P. (1994) 'Constructing scientific knowledge in the classroom', *Educational Researcher*, **23**, 7, pp. 5–12.

Driver, R., Guesne, E. and Tiberghien, A. (1985) *Children's Ideas in Science*. Milton Keynes, Open University.

Gardner, H. (1991) *The Unschooled Mind. How Children Think and How Schools Should Teach*. London, Basic Books – Fontana.

Gipps, C. (1999) 'Socio-cultural aspects of assessment', *Review of Research in Education*, **24**, pp. 355–94, AERA Washington DC.

Gipps, C., Brown, M., McCallum, B. and McAlister, S. (1995) *Intuition or Evidence? Teachers and National Assessment of Seven-Year Olds*. Buckingham, Open University Press.

Hattie, J. (1999) 'Influences on student learning', *The International Principal*, **5**, 3, pp. 7–9.

Krueger, R. A. (1994) *Focus Groups: A Practical Approach for Applied Research*. (2nd ed.) London, Sage.

Lucas, B. (2000) Towards a learning age, *Guardian Education*, 14 April 2000, p. 3.

Medwell, J., Wray D., Poulson, L. and Fox, R. (1998) *Effective Teachers of Literacy*. Final Report to TTA, School of Education, Exeter.

Ofsted (1999) *The National Literacy Strategy. An Evaluation of the First Year*. Ofsted, London, Ref HMI 216.

Pollard, A. (1990) 'Towards a sociology of learning in primary school', *British Journal of Sociology of Education*, **11**, 3, pp. 241–256.

Pollard, A., Broadfoot, P., Croll, P., Osborn, M. and Abbott, D. (1994) *Changing English Primary Schools: The Impact of the Education Reform Act at KS1*. London, Cassell.

Resnick, L. (1989) Introduction to: *Knowing, Learning and Instruction: Essays in honour of R. Glaser*, Resnick, L. (ed.). New Jersey, Lawrence Erlbaum.

Reynolds, D. (1997) 'East – West trade off', *Times Educational Supplement*. 26 June 1997, p. 21.

Rosenshine, B. and Stevens, R. (1986) 'Teaching functions', in *Handbook of Research on Teaching: 3rd ed*. Wittrock, M. (ed.) AERA Macmillan Publishing.

Rudduck, J., Chaplain, R. and Wallace, G. (1996) *School Improvement. What Can Pupils Tell Us?*. London, David Fulton.

Sadler, R. (1989) 'Formative assessment and the design of instructional systems'. *Instructional Science*, 18, pp. 119–44.

Sadler, R. (1998) 'Formative assessment: revisiting the territory', *Assessment in Education*, **5**, 1, pp. 77–84.

Torrance, H. and Pryor, J. (1998) *Investigating Formative Assessment: Teaching, Learning and Assessment in the Classroom*. Buckingham, England, Open University Press.

Tunstall, P. and Gipps, C. (1996) 'Teacher feedback to young children: A typology', *BERJ*, **22**, 4, pp. 389–404

Vygotsky, L. S. (1978) *Mind in Society. The Development of Higher Psychological Processes*. (eds) Cole, M., John-Steiner, V., Scribner, S. and Souberman, E. Cambridge, Harvard University Press.

Wragg, E. (1993) *Primary Teaching Skills*. London, Routledge.

Appendix
Research design

THE SAMPLE

We did not use test scores or measured progress over an academic year to select teachers as did the two TTA studies of *effective* teachers referred to in Chapter 1. There were several reasons for this. First, raw national assessment scores would not be an adequate identifier of good teaching because of the relationship of social class and previous educational experience to pupil performance. To overcome this, we would have had to use value-added scores and we did not have access to such data for individual teachers. Second, the use of gain scores over a school year to identify effective teachers would have required a bigger sample and more research time that we had available. (In this design a sample of teachers is followed over a year and the effective ones identified at the end; the effective teachers' practice is then compared with the less effective teachers' practice in a retrospective analysis. This type of design requires a large sample.) Third, we were interested in practice rather than output: our focus was on how teachers in different settings used a range of pedagogic strategies. We took as a given that expert teachers would have children's learning and academic progress as key targets. Many of the teachers were uncomfortable at being described as expert (and indeed one of the LEAs refused to use that term – other than privately in the selection of the sample). We, therefore, tended to use the terms 'good' or 'experienced' when we communicated with schools and teachers. However, in this book we refer to 'expert' teachers.

In May 1997 the selection of schools and teachers took place. Each LEA was asked to identify an initial 'purposive' sample of six Y2 and six Y6 teachers who were deemed to be 'expert', giving 24 teachers in all. To make a selection of teachers, the chief inspector in LEA 1 discussed possible schools with area advisers, inspectors and area education officers. In LEA 2, the chief inspector discussed possible schools with his team of general advisers. As part of their discussions advisers and inspectors in both LEAs considered recent inspections either they themselves or Ofsted had made of schools, as well as contributions particular schools had made to in-service training. Chief inspectors then approached headteachers of suggested schools and discussed the selection of teachers.

When selecting Y2 and Y6 teachers, LEAs and heads used the following criteria which had been negotiated with us, the researchers:

- graded 1 or 2 on Ofsted schedules during LEA inspections;
- is deemed to be expert on the basis of head's monitoring of teaching, perhaps leading to the award of responsibility points for being an outstanding teacher;
- has subject expertise, for example, is a subject co-ordinator for English, maths or science.

Individual teachers were then approached by heads and inspectors and asked to take part in the study.

Some examples of the bases for selection are:

- Chief inspector's knowledge from inspection: very experienced, very sound teacher plus head's observations; clear well-defined aims and learning intentions; calm; uses group work well.
- Area adviser's knowledge plus head's observations: very caring and thorough; good classroom ethos; good use of questioning and feedback; makes children think.
- Chief inspector's knowledge of school plus HMI (school has come out of 'special measures' status) and head's observations: lessons have a purpose and pace; assesses work, evaluates lessons and prepares next steps on the basis of this; looks at the learning outcomes, not just the teaching objectives.
- Area adviser's knowledge of the school plus good Ofsted report and head's observations: teacher received Ofsted 'excellent' teacher certificate; very well organised and planned; gains children's interest and confidence; trains helpers well; encourages critical skills in children.

The teachers

The final sample contained two men and 22 women. The gender imbalance is a little disappointing but not surprising; at nursery and

Table 1 Length of teacher experience

No. of years	1–5	6–10	11–15	16–20	21–25	25–30	over 30
No. of teachers	7	6	2	4	3	0	2

Table 2 Experience in different phases

Age phase	Infants/ Juniors/ Secondary	Juniors/ Secondary	Infant/ Secondary	Infants/ Juniors	Only Infants	Only Juniors
No. of teachers	1	1	1	10	6	5

primary school level the gender ratio of teachers for 1997 (the year in which these teachers were selected) was 17 per cent male to 83 per cent female (DfEE, 1998, Database of Teacher Records, Table 21). Years of teaching experience of teachers in the sample ranged widely as did experience of teaching different phases as Tables 1 and 2 show.

Interestingly, almost a third of the sample had been teaching for five years or less, indicating that long experience was not seen as a necessary aspect of 'expert' teachers. Two of the teachers were mature entrants who had joined the profession within the last five years.

The schools

In LEA 1, each teacher came from a different school and so there were 12 research schools. In LEA 2, some schools contained both a Y2 and Y6 teacher, while others contained only one; as a result there were eight research schools in LEA 2.

As it transpired, the 20 research schools represented a wide range of size and school type as Tables 3 and 4 illustrate:

Table 3 Size of school

No. of research schools	No. on roll
2	100–200
6	200–300
7	300–400
3	400–500
2	500+

Table 4 School types

No. of research schools	Type of school
1	Church Infant School (age 5–7)
5	LEA Infant Schools (age 5–7)
4	LEA Junior Schools (age 5–11)
2	Church Primary Schools (age 7–11)
8	LEA Primary Schools (age 7–11)

The schools were located in four very different geographical settings: suburban, town, inner-city and rural, representing a wide range of socio-economic and cultural backgrounds. For example, percentages of children on free school meals ranged across schools from 5 per cent to 65 per cent; percentages of SEN children (including statemented) ranged from 8 per cent to 45 per cent and percentages of ethnic minorities ranged from less than 1 per cent to 80 per cent. Some catchment areas contained predominantly owner-occupied housing, some mainly local authority housing, and some a mixture of both.

These groupings and variations went across both LEAs with the exception of percentage of free school meals and percentage of ethnic minorities, both of which were considerably higher in LEA 2. The percentage identified as having SEN was, conversely, higher in LEA 1. The wide range of the school sample is important, since it reassures us that these teachers were not all working in similar, or indeed privileged, settings. This lends credibility to any general trends or themes that emerge from the data.

The case study sample

The case study teachers were selected for more in-depth study than was possible with a sample of 23. Five teachers were excluded from the selection process: one of the two male teachers had moved on to become a head teacher and four teachers did not wish to be under more detailed scrutiny. The team wrote thumbnail sketches of each of the 18 remaining teachers and discussed in detail which ones to select, bearing in mind: teachers' organisational strategies; behaviour management and classroom relationships; main teaching strategies; assessment strategies; feedback strategies; approaches in different subjects; reflectiveness and articulateness; practice as consistent with responses in interview; links described or observed among teaching, assessment and feedback.

Our original plan was to visit 12 case study teachers, but on the advice of our advisory committee we reduced this to a more manageable 10 and decided that, although we should have five Y2 and five Y6 teachers we did not need to choose five from each LEA: we were interested in a range of strategies and the teacher's ability to talk about these, rather than LEA practice.

The teachers finally selected for (and who agreed to take part in) the case studies included one man and nine women; four from LEA 1 and six from LEA 2; three were in inner city areas, two were in council housing estates, one was in a rural setting, two suburban, one was described as having a catchment area of mostly owner-occupiers and one mostly professional middle class. This range of settings is matched by the range of approaches these teachers used. We included two teachers with classes that were difficult to manage; teachers who could talk about theory and those who found it difficult; teachers who had a traditional didactic relationship with children and teachers who construed that relationship in a more negotiating and constructing way.

Field work

From September to December 1997 we paid two-day visits to 23 teachers (one Y2 teacher had become seriously ill) to observe up to three lessons in each classroom. In Y2 we asked to observe reading, writing and maths and in Y6 English, maths and science. Afterwards we carried out post-observation interviews and the Four Card activity.

From March to April 1998, a further two-day visit was made to 10 case study teachers when we observed two lessons in each classroom, one in which teachers were introducing new subject content and one in which children were practising something already taught. During this visit teachers also took part in the Quote Sort activity.

From May to June 1998 we paid a further visit to non-case study teachers to carry out the Quote Sort activity with them. By then the overall sample was 22 as one Y6 teacher had left their school.

In September 1998 we held Focus Group interviews in both LEAs. Focus groups were conducted, recorded and analysed according to the methodology suggested by Krueger (1994) using a moderator and note-takers. Teachers were invited to discuss issues of teaching, assessment and feedback in a group situation. This offered an opportunity for validation of some of the strategies arising from our analysis. Further validation, in the Spring of 1999, was carried out with teachers in the study, other teachers in the project schools and teachers studying for higher degrees.

Asking the teachers about learning

We broached the subject of learning theory with teachers in three ways:

- in an open-ended way, in first interviews, we asked them what had been the greatest influences upon their practice;

- in a more focused way in later visits as part of the Quote Sort, we presented them with a teacher's direct quotes for discussion (e.g. 'You get a lot of theories at college, like Piaget and all those, but they are not much use when you get into the classroom');

- in the Four Cards activity in which we presented them with four statements about different theories of learning, and asked whether they agreed or disagreed with any (if they agreed they were asked about any implications for teaching);

- in the focus group, we specifically asked them to discuss cognitive views of learning versus social construction of knowledge, asking 'Does learning take place in the head or in the individual in social interaction?'.

Interviewing the pupils

We had not planned originally to talk to the pupils in any systematic way, but half-way into the fieldwork we decided to pilot some techniques for getting children to talk about learning. We used a version of the Four Cards activity (see above) which we had found helpful in getting teachers to talk about complex or unarticulated issues, within an open-ended interview setting. In the spring of 1998, we asked 10 case study teachers to ask children if they would be willing to take part in an interview and 23 Y6 and 21 Y2 children volunteered.

In the Four Cards Activity, we presented children with four statements about learning (distilled versions/loose representations of different learning theories). Each statement was written on a separate card and 'clip art' pictures were added to stimulate talk. Children were seen in a small group (of two to four); after discussing the four statements they were invited to give us their own statement, or fifth card. The sessions were taped and transcribed.

Index

Note: References to figures and tables are denoted by *f* and *t*.